# WITNESSES THROUGH TRIAL

## ORION

### Books in this series:

# WITNESSES THROUGH TRIAL

By MARVIN MOORE

Southern Publishing Association, Nashville, Tennessee

**Library of Congress Cataloging in Publication Data**

Moore, Marvin, 1937-
    Witnesses through trial.

    I. Title.
PZ7.M78716Wi              78-24294
ISBN 0-8127-0216-6

# CONTENTS

# INTRODUCTION

It was Tertullian who said, "The blood of the martyrs is the seed of the church." Whether or not it ends in death, Christian suffering has, through the centuries, been one of the most effective means of witnessing for Christ. The noble example of Christians who endured has turned men and women of all races and all cultures to Christ. Nor is the witness of God's suffering people less when unconverted hearts refuse to acknowledge it. The home can be as effective a forum for patient endurance as the prison cell. Even in a Christian home, within the church itself, nobly coping with the vicissitudes of life has proved an encouragement to others of like faith.

This book is a collection of eight stories of men, women, children, who experienced suffering and, through their endurance, witnessed to others. Most are in a modern setting. Some took place several hundred years ago, and one dates back two thousand years. But time has nothing to do with the drama, the miracle of witnessing for Christ under duress. The story of the three Hebrews in the flam-

ing furnace has lost none of its force with time, nor
will any of these.

I hope that these stories will provide interesting
Sabbath reading for young people and for adults of
all ages. But I especially hope that someone will
learn how to endure his own trials a little more
patiently, thus sharing his own Christian faith
more effectively. If this happens, then the witness
through trial of the characters in these stories will
continue as long as people read this book.

Marvin Moore

# TRIAL BY FIRING SQUAD*

I stood in the gravel pit by the pump house, shovel in hand, words of refusal still bitter on my lips. The sergeant's voice shook with anger.

"Either you shovel that pile of gravel or my firing squad shoots!" He shook his fist in my face. "We teach soldiers to obey orders seven days a week in this army, if it's the last thing we do to 'em!"

The knots in my stomach tightened. The officer whirled and marched straight for his riflemen. My mind clawed for some clue that this was not the end. Was he bluffing? The crescents his heels chopped in the hot summer dirt didn't leave much room for that. Huge muscles bulged on his neck. He barked an order, then whirled again. His arm flew up and a pudgy finger pointed straight at my face. My fingers tightened around the shovel.

---

*This story is an experience of William Clifford Cleveland (the father of Elder E. E. Cleveland, who was for many years an associate director in the Ministerial Department of the General Conference of Seventh-day Adventists in Washington, D.C.).

Eyes clamped shut, ears tensed for him to say the last words I would ever hear, I waited. Heavy footsteps pounded back my way. I forced my eyes open, then wished I hadn't.

"Shoot, white man, shoot!" my mind screamed.

He moved in, eyeball-to-eyeball. Beads of sweat on his forehead dripped onto mine. I felt his heart pound. His tobacco-stained breath blasted the order through my nose: "Soldier! Move that shovel!" Then he backed off and glared.

Confusion fogged me in as my brain whirled. "God," I breathed. And then I knew what to do. For a few seconds I looked at him. Then I held the shovel out to him. "Shoot me if you wish," I told him, "but I cannot do what you ask."

His jaw dropped. Disbelief broke through the rage on his face. Fire shot from his eyes as they met mine for a second. Turning to his men, he sent them on their way with a wave of his hand, then glared at me again. "Soldier," he bellowed, "the CO wants to see you at 1600 hours at headquarters. Now get to your barracks!"

After what seemed an endless walk past taunts and jeers of "holy-day boy," and "Advent Sabbathkeeper," I finally reached the barracks. I sank down on my bunk, relieved to be alone in the empty room. "God," I cried, "where are You? You worked everything out so perfectly last week. How did this happen?"

To the Adventist evangelist who baptized me that Sabbath morning late in 1916, the World War was mainly a sign of the end. Few Americans felt personally involved. Hadn't our President promised to keep us out of war? Then suddenly we were fighting in it. Wondering just how my new faith would fit in with Uncle Sam's army, I obeyed my summons to serve.

But God was on my side. Without speaking to a single officer about my Sabbath, I simply prayed and hoped. And God had honored my trust. Early that first Sabbath morning an officer called us all out to the parade grounds for a surprise inspection. One bold exception stood out among the wrinkled batch of GI's that straggled out and lined up: me!

"One thing you guys had better learn in this army, and fast!" the officer barked, "and that is that you are *always* ready for inspection. Out of this whole lousy bunch, only one man is ready. Congratulations, Cleveland. You may take the day off. There's a pass waiting for you at headquarters. The rest of you punks report for work at 900 hours."

The poor officer was quite unaware that I had prepared for church, *not* for his inspection. Man, what a God! With Him on my side, army life would be a snap.

And now this. Sitting up on my bunk, I tried to think through the morning events. I searched for an answer, but like a whirlpool, my dazed brain sucked every snatch of hope out of reach.

When I turned to lie down again, my face brushed against something. I pushed it aside, then realized that I held my Bible. Sitting up, I turned to the story of Daniel in the lions' den. With new courage I leafed back to Psalms. There I found my answer: "Call upon me in the day of trouble: I will deliver thee, and thou shalt glorify me" (Psalm 50:15). Sinking to my knees I claimed God's promise.

A moment later I heard loud, explosive talk coming my way. I tensed to jump to my feet, when a voice spoke up: "That'll teach him to spruce up for his Sabbath and put us to work all day, while he goes out and has a lark. Time we get through with his sand bath, he won't be sittin', standin', or lyin' for a week!"

With the Bible open on the bed in front of me, I stayed on my knees. Feet hit the front steps and the door flew open. In walked about half a dozen of my buddies. I knew they could hardly wait to get their hands on me. The room became deathly silent. For a moment not a man moved. Then I heard whispers and the sound of feet tiptoeing from the barracks.

God *was* still on my side. He had spared me a rubdown with sand by men who were so angry that they would have left my body one solid abrasion. After a prayer of thanksgiving I sat down again and searched the Bible for texts to memorize in preparation for my interview with the commanding officer.

A few hours later, Bible in hand, I went to the headquarters building. A private pecked at a typewriter on a desk in the middle of the room. He stopped long enough to hear my name and motion me to a chair on my right. I sat down beside what I concluded must be the door to the commander's office.

As I sat there the starkness of the place, bare

except for the necessities, depressed me. A lone bulb dangled from a long twist of black wire that ran up one corner of the room and out to the center of the ceiling. Dusty racks of military and World War propaganda guarded either side of the door I had just entered. Across the room, skewed at an irritating angle, hung a picture of President Woodrow Wilson. Under the windows along the back wall stood a couple of old desks and an antique filing cabinet. A clock between the windows announced the time: 3:45. I had purposely arrived early.

Settling back to wait, I felt new peace wash over me. The fog, the confusion of the morning, vanished. For several minutes I sat there, eyes shut, praying. Then the commanding officer's door flew open and out burst two distraught junior officers. I jerked my feet in as they rushed past. The commander, General Andrew Stanfield, strode out the door after them.

"Where's Cleveland!" he demanded. "Isn't it enough he disobeyed orders this morning without being late to see me? Get him here!"

Scarcely glancing up, the private at the typewriter nodded in my direction. "He's right over there, sir."

General Stanfield turned and glared at me. "Black boy," he said, "don't you know that 1600 hours means 4:00? Look at that clock, and next time be here three minutes early!"

The clock said 3:57. "Yes, sir," I mumbled.

The commander closed the door and walked

back to his large mahogany desk. On the wall above him hung a picture of the President flanked by two flags. He motioned to a chair in front of the desk. "Sit there."

He paused. I waited. After shifting in his chair, he growled, "Cleveland, they tell me you disobeyed orders this morning and talked back at an officer. What do you have to say for yourself?" Leaning back in his large swivel chair, he eyed me through a haze of cigar smoke.

I pulled in my stomach. "The sergeant told me to shovel gravel on the Sabbath, sir." Wondering which showed through most, my waning courage or my jitters, I added, "But I was not aware of talking back at him. I am sorry if I did."

General Stanfield leaned forward. His eyes glared into mine. "In this army, Cleveland, any time you refuse to obey an order, you're talking back. And as for that Sabbath of yours, this is the army, not church. We don't know what the Sabbath is, and what's more, we aren't interested in finding out."

He paused, reached for a pen and paper, and began to write. After a couple of lines he looked up. "Now, young man," he continued, his voice barely softer, "I'm not going to do anything about this morning's incident. But next Saturday morning you'd better do what you're told or you'll be in for *real* trouble. Is that clear?"

"God, what do I say now?" I breathed. The story of the three Hebrews before the enraged Nebuchadnezzar flashed across my mind. I looked up. "Sir, I understand what you said and why you said it. But I cannot work on God's Sabbath. It begins at sundown on Friday and ends at sundown on Saturday. I'll be glad to do double duty any other time, but it will be impossible for me to work on the Sabbath."

The officer half rose from his chair, eyes flashing through slits and his face reddening. Jaw set, he leaned toward me. His fist slammed the table. "Soldier!" he bellowed. "What kind of army do you think this would be if every man in it told us what he was and wasn't going to do and when he planned to do it? Next Friday night, or Saturday morning, you'll do what you're told!" He shook his head violently.

"Sir, it's not that I won't. I can't. My Bible teaches me that God's law is above every human law, and the Sabbath is one of His laws. I *must* obey God."

General Stanfield settled back into his chair. "Private Cleveland," he said tersely, "you are under military arrest. Report to this office for court-martial in three days, at this same time. Till then, stay in your barracks. That is all." Rising, he motioned toward the door. I stood to leave.

He reached for the knob, only to turn and face me again. "Your meals will be brought to you." Then he glanced at my Bible. "And bring along that book with *your* laws in it when you come back here," he commanded with icy scorn.

Three days later I sat again in General Stanfield's waiting room. Again I listened to the private—a different one this time—peck at the typewriter. Again I closed my eyes to the glare of the light bulb suspended overhead.

Pictures of the past couple of weeks drifted back and forth through my imagination. I thought of God's answer to my prayer that first Sabbath morning, how He gave me the day off without my even having to ask for it. I remembered the sergeant's terrifying bluff before a firing squad the next Sabbath, and of how He rescued me from a torturous sand bath a few minutes later. I thought of the tense interview with General Stanfield that afternoon and of the past three days that I had spent in Bible study and prayer, preparing for the afternoon court-martial.

Eventually I realized that perhaps God *was* answering my prayer for freedom to keep His Sabbath holy, but in a different way. After all, I was still alive. The authorities had not sent me to the guardhouse; they had trusted me to stay in my own quarters and to appear on time for the trial without sending a military policeman to escort me.

"Lord, I don't know what they'll do to me in there. I trust You to give me the right words so that this trial can be a witness for Your truth. Help me . . ."

Heavy footsteps interrupted my prayer. The sounds of joking and laughing came from just outside the front door. Seconds later, the door burst open, and the levity stopped. Three officers, severity on their faces, stepped to the private's desk. The private jumped to attention and saluted.

"We're here to see General Stanfield for a court-martial," a heavyset captain announced.

"The general said he would see you as soon as you arrive, sir." The private stepped to the door and knocked. After a pause, he entered. When he emerged, he addressed the captain again. "General Stanfield says he'll be with you in just a minute, sir."

"I hope he won't be too long," clipped a nervous second lieutenant. "I haven't got all day."

"You may be seated if you wish, sir," the private told him. "He's just signing a few documents."

The lieutenant took the chair next to mine, then edged away from me. I felt like poison. The others stood, blowing smoke about the room.

The front door swung open again, and another lieutenant hurried in. Shorter and stouter than the one beside me, he puffed and wiped his face with his handkerchief. "What's this all about, anyway?" he demanded. "They called me at the last minute, and I'm stacked to the gills with reports to get to Washington by Monday. I suppose this will make me one more." He shot a scornful glance my way.

"Aw, some recruit thinks he's going to baptize the U.S. Army into his church," spat a noncommissioned officer.

His statement jarred me out of what little composure I had left. I hadn't noticed that one of the officers in the room was the sergeant I'd met at the gravel pile three days before. He flipped a cigarette into an ashtray.

Just then General Stanfield appeared at his door.

The lieutenant next to me snapped to his feet. The others joined him in a smart salute. The commander brushed his hand to his forehead and motioned toward the door.

"We'll call for you when we're ready, Cleveland," General Stanfield said. He turned and closed the door behind him.

I waited for what seemed an eternity. When the door opened again, the sergeant ordered, "Private Cleveland, General Stanfield wants to see you in here."

Picking up my Bible, I went past the waiting sergeant into the room and saluted. Behind the desk sat the five white officers who would hear my case.

"You will be seated, Private Cleveland." General Stanfield waved toward the chair I had occupied three days earlier. I felt like the proverbial sheep among wolves.

The general cleared his throat. "Private Cleveland, this is Captain Smith and Lieutenant Carter on my left, and Lieutenant Hurst and Sergeant Spears on my right." I exchanged glances with the officers. "We understand," Stanfield continued, "that at about 900 hours last Saturday morning you refused to obey Sergeant Spears' order to work at the gravel pile by the pump house. Give an account of yourself."

"I'm happy to obey any order I'm given by a . . ."

"By an officer you *feel* like obeying, black boy!" shot back the sergeant. "You sure felt like obeying me last Saturday morning, didn't you?"

"Cleveland," Captain Smith joined in, "you either get that crazy religion out of your head or you'll be serving this army a whole lot longer than you started out to."

"Gentlemen," I replied, "my religion teaches me to obey my superiors, and that includes officers in the army. However, my religion also teaches me to——"

"Listen, soldier," cut in Lieutenant Hurst. "I haven't got all day to listen to you preach about your crazy religion. You're making me have to fill out one more report to send to Washington, as if all I had to do was send in reports on screwballs like you. *Will* you do what you are told, *when* you're told, or *won't* you? That's all Washington wants to know, and that's all I care to waste the ink to tell them."

"Cleveland, you may finish what you had to say," broke in General Stanfield. "We will listen." He leaned back in his chair and puffed on his cigar.

"Thank you, sir," I replied. "As I said, I do not wish to disobey my superiors. But as a Christian, I believe one must obey God rather than human authority anytime the two conflict. The Bible teaches that Saturday is the Sabbath, and it forbids any work on that day. That is why I could not do what Sergeant Spears ordered me to do last Saturday morning."

"Soldier," the captain demanded, "what outfit taught you this nonsense, anyway? Were your parents foolish enough to bring you up this way?"

"No, sir," I replied. "I have believed this for less

than a year. I am a Seventh-day Adventist. I——"

"A seven day how many?" Lieutenant Carter interrupted.

"Seventh-day Adventist," General Stanfield volunteered. He picked up a card and leaned toward Lieutenant Carter. "It's right here on his record. Go ahead, Cleveland," he said with a glance my way. He handed my card to the officer.

"I joined the Adventist Church of my own free will after hearing a series of Bible lectures in my hometown several months ago. Now I realize the problem I'm creating for you gentlemen, and I wish it didn't have to be this way. But I believe with all my heart that Saturday is the Sabbath, and I'm prepared to take the consequences, even if it means death."

"That's the ridiculous truth!" muttered the sergeant under his breath. His beady eyes met mine—the same eyes I'd seen the previous Sabbath morning at the gravel pit.

"I really don't care where you got this notion or who put it *into* your head," spat Captain Smith. "But I know who's going to get it *out!*"

"I wouldn't be too sure of that, sir," Spears growled. "You should have seen the idiot make a fool of himself last Saturday morning—excuse me, Private, Sabbath morning," he added in mock respect.

There was a pause. Tension filled the room. My stomach convulsed.

"Your church teaches you to rebel against the government!" exploded Lieutenant Carter. "Rebellion! That's all it is, rebellion, pure and simple." He half stood and shook his fist at me. "Maybe you *will* die before this is settled"—his voice rose to a near scream—"Die over some fool notion."

Staring at my feet, I silently asked God what to do. At last I decided there wasn't anything I could do. So I sat there with my head bowed, my five white tormentors glaring at me.

General Stanfield broke the silence. "Gentlemen," he said, rising to his feet, "I think Private Cleveland's position is quite clear to all of us. That is what I wanted you to hear. I will have to think this case through some more before I make a decision. I know you are all busy with other responsibilities; so you may be excused." The four rose to leave. The company commander stepped ahead to open the door and said, "Lieutenant Carter, I'll make out the report to Washington on this incident myself."

"Yes, sir, thank you, sir," the lieutenant replied. The men left the room. I leaned forward to stand, but the general stopped me with a wave of his hand.

The door closed again. General Stanfield returned to his chair behind the desk. Feeling his searching look fixed on me, I glanced at him out of the corner of my eye and wondered what he was thinking. His face appeared serious, but he didn't seem angry. For several minutes he sat, scarcely moving, just thinking. He rubbed his chin with his fingers. Presently he got up. Taking Sergeant Spears' chair, he brought it around the desk and set it down close to mine.

"Cleveland," he began—I noticed a touch of kindness in his voice— "the army isn't opposed to you fellows going to church on Sunday from time to time. You want it on Saturday, and that could be arranged. But you're different. You insist that it has got to be *every* Saturday, and not just services in the morning either, but the whole day, starting on Friday night. I told you to bring that Book with you when you came to see me. Now I want you to show me from the Bible where it says *that*."

With a prayer that the Lord would guide my mind, I began with the story of Creation. Moving through to the experience of the children of Israel, I explained the fourth commandment and the sacredness of the day. I pointed out God's intention of blessing a specific day as seen in His threefold miracle of the manna for forty years. In the New Testament I pointed out the example of Christ and the apostles. The commander's interest seemed genuine. Finally I concluded with the prophecy about Sabbathkeeping in the new earth in the last chapter of Isaiah.

"Young man, I can see that you know what you believe. I'd like to know what you people teach about war."

With another prayer for help, I did the best I could to explain. When we finished with war, he wanted to know about the second coming of Christ, then about death, the resurrection, the judgment, the millennium, and hell. The kind of questions he asked gave me the distinct impression he knew more about Seventh-day Adventists than he cared to reveal and that he was testing me to see what *I* knew. We sat for an hour, covering nearly every phase of the church's belief. With each passing moment, his attitude became more favorable.

Finally he stood to his feet and put out his hand. "Cleveland," he said, "I congratulate you on knowing so well what you believe. For one so recently baptized into your faith, I am frankly amazed at the extent of your knowledge. I know about Seventh-day Adventists. They are good people. My family employs a Seventh-day Adventist maid, and she gives us honest, faithful service. Don't you worry about that report to Washington. It will be favorable, I can assure you. And don't worry about your Sabbath, either. As long as you are under my command, the time is yours from sundown Friday till sundown Saturday."

Relief flooded over me. I felt weak, but I managed to salute and say, "Yes, sir, thank you, sir!"

The officer walked with me to the door and held it open. "Oh, one more thing"—and when he touched my arm to stop me, I turned and looked at him, noticing a twinkle in his eye—"mind you, don't go teaching that religion of yours around here too much, or we won't have any army left!"

# UNDER THE OPEN WINDOW

Anna wriggled her toes in the sand and dropped her hands to her side to keep her dress from blowing in the brisk sea breeze. Her dark-brown eyes, half filled with awe, sparkled nonetheless as she watched Pastor Thurmon break away from the crowd. A low murmur rose from the three hundred or so people on the beach as the pastor stepped over to a thin young girl, about twelve years old, and led her down to the water. Their black robes whipped in the breeze and billowed around them as they walked slowly into the sea.

Her mind drifting back across the past few months, Anna thought of the Bible lessons Rebecca had received in the mail each week. She remembered the awe with which everyone in Coral Bay Village looked at Rebecca ever since the day Pastor Thurmon called on her. And she especially remembered Sister Minerva's visit and how angry the old woman had been. It all seemed as though it had happened only yesterday.

She had crouched in a corner of her home, hardly daring to breathe. Sister Minerva had sat in the chair that Anna's father placed in the center of the room. The dim light coming through the window made the woman's wrinkled face look older than ever, Anna thought. She felt almost amused at her long nose that dropped to a hook at the end.

"I only came to stay a minute," the woman cackled.

Anna couldn't remember a time when she hadn't heard that voice about the village streets, warning the people against sin, admonishing them to be faithful to the church.

"I want to know whether you can tell me about the little girl who is staying with the heretics next door—the Martins," Sister Minerva began.

Anna's father answered. "My daughter has been a friend of Rebecca's since she came to live with her aunt and uncle a few months ago."

The old woman turned and fixed her attention on Anna. The girl trembled and crouched farther in the corner.

"I understand that Rebecca has tuberculosis," Sister Minerva commented. "Is she very sick?"

"We used to play in the Martins' house, and sometimes even outside when she first came," Anna faltered. "But the past few weeks she has been too sick even to get out of bed. I heard Mrs. Martin say yesterday that she hardly even eats anymore. The doctor will see her tomorrow when he comes to the village."

Sister Minerva paused before her next question. "And is it true that the Martins have been taking Rebecca to the Adventist services on Saturday?"

"Oh, no! I mean, yes," Anna gasped. "The first few weeks she was here, they took her with them every Saturday. But recently she's been too sick to go."

"And did she enjoy it? I mean, was she being influenced by it?"

The girl glanced down and wriggled her toes in the dirt of the floor. "Well," she half whispered, "she asked me to go with her once."

"Those heretics! The child's mother should never have allowed her to come and live with them."

"Oh, but Rebecca's father died in a storm at sea," Anna protested. "With ten other children, Rebecca's mother couldn't take care of her."

"It's better to die than to be turned into a heretic!" Sister Minerva replied, then stood and turned to Anna's father. "I shall appreciate a report from you on the results of the doctor's visit. Perhaps you can allow Anna to go to their home long enough to find out about that. Then I shall call on Rebecca myself." She turned and left as suddenly as she had come.

All that night Anna slept fitfully, thinking and dreaming about the doctor's visit the next day. She dreamed of heretics burning in hell, of saints singing in heaven, and through it all she wondered where Rebecca and the Martins belonged. They were so kind and helpful, always smiling. The girl had a hard time believing that people like that would burn forever.

Anna was glad the next morning for an excuse to

spend an hour at the Martins' before the doctor arrived. Not having seen Rebecca for more than a week, she gasped when she stepped through the door into her room. Rebecca, coughing quietly, lay on her cot. The skin hung from the bones on her arms and legs, and the shape of her teeth showed through her cheeks. Her eyes seemed sunken back into her head. A breeze from the sea drifted through the open window across the room. Rebecca barely managed a weak smile when Anna stepped to her bedside and stroked her hair.

An hour later Mrs. Martin led the doctor into the room. "How is my little patient this morning?" he asked as he set his black bag down by Rebecca's bed.

The girl nodded and coughed again.

The doctor took Rebecca's temperature and touched his fingers to her wrist to count her heartbeat. He drew a stethoscope from his bag and listened to Rebecca's chest. Rebecca's ribs reminded Anna of the carcasses of animals she had seen by the sea.

When he finished his examination, the physician motioned for Rebecca's aunt and uncle to follow him into another room. Anna heard them talking in low tones. When they returned a few minutes later, she saw tears in Mrs. Martin's eyes. The doctor stepped to the patient's side. "Rebecca," he said gently, stroking her face.

She nodded.

"You know that you have tuberculosis, don't you?"

The girl nodded again.

The doctor paused. "You are a very sick little girl, my dear. Your aunt and uncle asked me to tell you how sick you really are."

Rebecca looked into his eyes.

"I don't think you have long to live." Anna noticed that he spoke each word deliberately. "I'm afraid the disease has gone too far to do anything about it." He patted her on the shoulder. Then he left the room.

Anna watched the lids close over Rebecca's eyes. A tear trickled down the side of her face, and she sighed and murmured. "Jesus is the only One who can make me well now," she whispered.

Mrs. Martin knelt beside her niece. "My dear," she said in a choked voice, "Pastor Thurmon will be in Coral Bay Village tomorrow for Sabbath School and church. I'm going to ask him to come and pray for you before he leaves."

Her heart pounding, Anna wondered if Rebecca would let the Martins bring a heretic to pray for her.

Rebecca glanced up. "Ask the juniors from my Sabbath School class to come with him," she requested softly.

Mrs. Martin nodded. "I know they will be glad to."

Anna's throat tightened, and the muscles in her arms and legs tensed. Her eyes darted about the room. "I—I—I must be going now," she stammered. "I—I can't stay any longer." She fled through the small house and into the sunshine outside. The cool sea breeze blew against her cheeks, and she felt as though she had suddenly awakened from another horrible dream. Hardly seeing where she ran, she almost stumbled across her father, who sat mending his fishnet on the front steps of their home.

"Not so fast, my child," he chided. "How is it that you are so out of breath this early in the day?"

"Oh, Father!" Anna exclaimed. "I just saw something terrible. You must tell Sister Minerva at once!"

He sprang to his feet. "What is it?" he demanded.

"The Adventist minister is coming after their church service tomorrow to pray for Rebecca, and she asked the Martins to bring the children too."

"Yes, I must tell Sister Minerva!" He hurried up the lane that wound between the homes in the village.

All afternoon Anna wondered whether Sister Minerva would arrive in time the next day to save Rebecca. She told several of her friends what had happened. Some of them had already heard the story. By evening the entire village buzzed with the news.

The next morning Anna watched the Martins leave for church. Would Sister Minerva come while they were gone? She breathed a sigh of relief when they returned at noon without the pastor or the children. "Sister Minerva still has time to save Rebecca," she whispered to herself.

Almost as though someone had told her they were home again, the old woman trudged up the village lane toward the Martins' house less than five minutes after they returned. Anna noticed that her eyes gleamed. Her lips were set in a tight line. She pounded on the front door. Groups of people gathered about the front of the house to watch. Anna slipped around to the back and crouched under Rebecca's open window.

"Rebecca," she heard Mrs. Martin call a few minutes later, "Sister Minerva is here to see you." Mrs. Martin's voice sounded pleasant, Anna thought, as though she were bringing a friend to visit. She heard Rebecca's faint "hello."

"Rebecca," Sister Minerva began, her voice low and gentle. "I'm an old, old woman. God is going to take me one of these days. Do you know where I'll go when I die?"

A long pause followed. Curious to know what was happening inside, Anna rose slowly and peeked over the edge of the window. "Oh!" she gasped, then clapped her hand over her mouth.

The sick girl still lay on the bed, but she had propped herself up on one elbow, facing Sister Minerva. "You're not talking about *you* dying," Rebecca said in a clear voice. "You're talking about *me* dying. Well, I'm not going to die. The pastor and the children from the Adventist Church are coming to pray for me this afternoon, and God is going to make me well again for a witness to this village."

The old woman glared at Rebecca. "You little heretic!" she shrieked. "The devil's got hold of you, and you're going to die. When you do, you aren't going to heaven either. God will punish you in hell!" She stalked out of the room.

Anna dashed around the corner of the house just in time to see her emerge from the door. Dusting her feet on a mat, the old woman surveyed the villagers gathered in front of the house. "The child's a heretic!" she cried. "She's going to let the heretics pray for her, and she's going to die. God will punish her for her sins!" Pushing her way past the people, she rushed down the village lane.

Anxiously Anna waited to see what would happen next. Two hours later Pastor Thurmon and the children arrived. He carried a Bible in his hand and chatted with the children as he walked. Small groups of people clustered near the front of the house as before. Anna's father joined them. The girl slipped around to the back to listen.

"Rebecca," she heard Mrs. Martin call a moment later. "Pastor Thurmon and the children are here to see you."

"Hello, Rebecca," the pastor said. "The children and I came to pray for you this afternoon. Do you believe God can make you well?"

Rebecca replied weakly. The pastor read a passage from the Bible, then he requested the children to kneel. One by one they asked God to make Rebecca well. "Dear Jesus," one little girl prayed, "please make Rebecca strong again so she can come to Sabbath School and learn to love You more. Amen."

After the children had prayed, Pastor Thurmon began: "Father in heaven, Jesus died to save us from the power of Satan. Rebecca has been under

Satan's power with this disease, and so now we come asking You to deliver her. . . .

*Sister Minerva said the heretics would turn Rebecca over to the devil,* Anna thought. *She didn't say they would deliver her from him!*

"Rebecca's body is sick," Pastor Thurmon continued. "Please take this sickness from her as You took the sickness from Jairus' little girl when You were on earth. And now, Rebecca, as the Bible commands, I anoint you with this oil that God may forgive your sins and heal your disease."

Slowly Anna peeked over the edge of the window—just in time to see Pastor Thurmon touch the index finger of his right hand to Rebecca's forehead. He held a small bottle in his left hand.

When Pastor Thurmon had finished praying, he and the children rose to their feet and sang. Anna noticed that Rebecca's feet moved. She seemed to be trying to get them over the edge of the bed.

Pastor Thurmon changed the song. "Praise God from whom all blessings flow!" he began in a clear, strong voice. All the children joined in. "Praise Him all creatures here below." Mrs. Martin knelt by Rebecca's side and wept.

The last words of the song faded away. For several seconds nobody spoke. Anna dropped to her knees again and listened. Rebecca broke the silence with, "I'm hungry."

"Bring her something to eat," Pastor Thurmon told Mrs. Martin. "The Bible says that Jesus told Jairus to give his daughter something to eat after He healed her."

Anna waited till she heard Mrs. Martin return before she peeked over the edge of the window again. She saw Rebecca eating, and then she hurried back to the front of the house. "She's well! Rebecca's well!" she exclaimed. She ran to her father and grasped his hand.

"She can't be!" he declared. "Sister Minerva said she'd die."

"But she *is* well," Anna insisted. "I heard them pray, and then I saw Rebecca sit up. Mrs. Martin brought her some food, and she's eating it."

Everyone gathered around Anna and talked at once. Presently the Martins' front door opened and the crowd gasped. Pastor Thurmon stepped outside, leading Rebecca by the hand. The girl still looked as thin as before, but she held her head high as she walked slowly down the lane with her friends.

Anna's mind reviewed the weeks that followed, remembering how Rebecca had studied the Bible faithfully every day and how she had written to Pastor Thurmon, asking him to baptize her the next time he came to Coral Bay Village. She recalled how excited Rebecca had been just last Wednesday when she received Pastor Thurmon's letter telling her he would be in Coral Bay Village today.

Blinking her eyes as though she had awakened from a dream, Anna watched Pastor Thurmon hold his hand toward heaven as he stood in the sea. She saw him lower Rebecca gently into the water, then raise her again. After he had dried her face with a white handkerchief, he led her out of the sea. Pastor

Thurmon, crossing the sandy beach, stepped up to one of the villagers and spoke to him. They shook hands. Others soon crowded around. In back of the onlookers Anna spotted Sister Minerva. The woman cast a dark look at the people and disappeared into the village.

Anna found Rebecca standing beside her aunt and uncle. A blanket, one corner dragging in the sand, lay draped around her shoulders. Anna approached Rebecca and took her hand, squeezing it tight. The two girls smiled into each other's eyes.

# THE LAST WORDS YOU SPOKE

Stephen strode across the lawn in front of his new home and onto the street. A quarter mile down the road he found Philip trimming a hedge he had recently set out in front of his house. "Good morning, Philip," he called cheerfully.

"Good morning, yourself." Philip clapped a hand across his friend's broad shoulder. "And where might you be going in such a hurry?"

"Daniel invited me to a reception at his new place," Stephen said.

A wave of the hand, and the two friends parted. Winding another half mile down the slope, Stephen came upon a mansion set back in a tree-filled yard. He turned onto the path that led to it. A moment later he knocked at the heavy oak door.

"Well, good morning, good morning, and do come in!" exclaimed the stocky, white-haired man who opened the door. "I remember you. We met last Sabbath after the worship service." He put out his hand. The two men shook hands vigorously.

Daniel led the way across a white marble floor to a den in the back of the house. A large harp stood in one corner. Through an open door Stephen noticed what seemed to be a small study. The older man crossed in front of a couch to a sliding glass door, which he pulled open, and the two men stepped into a wide yard that stretched perhaps a hundred yards to a tall hedge at the back. Here and there oak and poplar trees shaded the lawn.

Stephen surveyed the little knots of people scattered about the yard. Under an oak tree he recognized a group of friends and started toward them. Halfway there, he stopped short and stared. His face pale, he stood rooted to the ground a moment, then whirled and rushed back to his host. "Daniel! Daniel!"

"Is something wrong?" Daniel asked.

"Where's the Teacher?"

Daniel surveyed the yard. "Over there. I think that's Him in the white coat, sitting under a poplar tree with those two men."

Stephen peered in the direction that Daniel pointed. "Yes, thank you," he blurted, hurrying across the lawn.

The Teacher sat cross-legged on the grass, visiting with His friends. He turned when Stephen touched His shoulder.

"Oh, hello, Stephen," the Teacher said cheerfully in His bass voice. "Is something the matter?" He asked, studying the man's face.

"Please," Stephen said, "I want to talk to You—alone."

"Why, yes, of course." Turning to His friends, He said, "Excuse Me just a moment, please."

The other man followed Stephen back toward the house. When they came near the group that Stephen had planned to join, the young man stopped and stared. The Teacher seemed puzzled. "Who is *that* man?" Stephen demanded. "The short one under the oak tree."

The Teacher looked in the direction Stephen pointed. A second later His face lit up, and He seemed almost amused. "That's Saul, Stephen."

"Not Saul of Tarsus!"

"Yes, Saul of Tarsus."

"I *thought* I recognized him," Stephen exclaimed. "But what is *he* doing here? The last time I saw him, he . . ."

Jesus took his arm. "Come with Me. I have something to show you that you've never seen before." He led the way to the house. Daniel saw them approaching and opened the door. "May I borrow that set of scrolls Matthew gave you a couple of days ago?" Jesus asked him.

"Of course, help Yourself. They're on the shelf in the other room." He motioned toward the study with his hand.

To the left as they entered the room stood two upholstered chairs. To the right, on a wide, deep shelf over a desk, lay several rolls of parchment.

"Take one," Jesus said.

Stephen reached for one of the loosely bound rolls. Opening it, he scanned it a moment, then glanced up. "This is an Isaiah scroll. I thought You were going to show me something I'd never seen before."

Jesus smiled. "Here, try this one." He took a small scroll from the stack on the shelf.

Laying it on the desk, Stephen gingerly felt for the edge of the sheet and rolled it open. "This one's in Greek!" he exclaimed. "The Gospel According to Mark." He looked at Jesus. " 'The gospel'—does that mean the Good News of salvation?"

"Yes. It's the story of My mission on earth."

Stephen studied the scroll a moment. "Oh, now I see. These are the sayings and stories that we memorized and taught to the people as we went from village to village. Mark wrote them down. An excellent idea! That wasn't John Mark, was it—that impulsive kid?"

Jesus chuckled. "Kids don't stay kids forever, you know. Mark became a great preacher. His was the first Gospel. Two others based their Gospels on his, and John wrote one too."

"This *is* interesting! Here, let me see more."

"Why don't we take several of them and sit in these chairs where we can be comfortable?" Jesus suggested. He chose three or four scrolls and carried them across the room. A moment later the two men sat with the scrolls laid out on the floor between them.

Stephen picked up a scroll, unrolled its curled edges, and studied the carefully shaped letters. "The Epistle of Paul to the Church at Rome," he read slowly. " 'Paul, a servant of Jesus Christ, called to be an apostle, separated unto the gospel . . .' " Stephen looked up at Jesus. "I never heard of an apostle Paul."

"That's Saul. Paul was his Gentile name."

"You mean *him*—Saul of Tarsus! He was one of Your apostles?"

The Teacher leaned forward. "You knew him only as a persecutor of the church. But I came to him one day, and he was never the same after that. Let Me show you something in his letter to the church at Galatia." Taking a thin scroll, Jesus scanned its columns and gave it to Stephen. "Here," He said, pointing with His finger.

Stephen read, " 'I am crucified with Christ: nevertheless I live; yet not I, but Christ liveth in me: and the life which I now live in the flesh I live by the faith of the Son of God, who loved me, and gave himself for me.' " He laid the scroll in his lap. "That's magnificent! And You mean Saul of Tarsus wrote that?"

"After he was converted," Jesus replied.

"I know it's true," Stephen said, shaking his head, "because the man is up here. But I can still hardly believe it. How did it happen?"

"It was the witness of your victorious death that did it." Jesus smiled. "That's what started him on the way."

"My *victorious* death?" Stephen eyed the Master carefully. "All my death did was to bring shame and reproach on the church."

"It seemed that way at first, but it was quite the opposite. Saul was never the same after that. He couldn't get it out of his mind, the way you took it so calmly."

Stephen sat thinking. His mind went back to the

bitter wrath of the Jewish leaders the day he stood before them in the council chamber and condemned them for crucifying the Saviour. Into his memory came the screams of madmen as they rushed from their seats. They tore at him with their hands and beat him with their fists. Shoving him from the council room, they dragged him down the streets of Jerusalem to the stoning pit outside the wall.

They threw their outer garments at the feet of Saul, and screaming, they hurled Stephen into the center of the pit. He hit the ground on his back.

The first stone cut through his nose and mouth. "Take this! And this! And this!" he heard them shriek through clenched teeth. Another stone tore into his right ear. Swiftly he rolled over. Stone after stone smashed into his head and back. Blood filled his mouth. Pain shot through his body in waves that wracked every nerve.

The thought flashed through his mind: "Traitors, murderers who killed the Lord!" He felt tempted to shriek a bitter condemnation at his tormentors. Then he remembered his Lord's example on the cross. "But how can I? They deserve fire and brimstone, not that!" he thought.

A fist-size stone smashed into his skull and nearly left him senseless. His fingers clutched the dust. "No! No! I can't!" Another huge stone in his back knocked the breath from his lungs. Again, a bitter denunciation nearly burst from his torn lips. But his mind flashed back to the Master on the cross. "Father!" he gasped. "Help me!" Mustering every ounce of energy left in his bruised body, he rose slowly, painfully to his knees, stones pounding at him from every direction.

"Lord!" he cried out. "Lay not this sin to their charge!" Then he could remember no more.

Stephen felt a hand on his shoulder. Jarred back to reality but still overcome with emotion, he looked into Jesus' eyes. His lips quivered.

"I understand," Jesus said as He knelt beside Stephen. "You see, I had to say the same thing Myself, on the cross. I too had to ask God to forgive My enemies."

His body trembling, Stephen bit his lip and shook his head. Tears streamed down his cheeks. "It was the hardest thing I ever did," he choked under his breath.

Jesus gripped his shoulder. "But that's what did it for Saul—the last words you spoke. He never could erase them from his mind. It was the last words you spoke that finally drove him to Me."

Stephen threw himself upon the Master's breast and wept bitterly for several minutes. At last he drew away. "And to think that I almost didn't," he whispered. "But for Saul, it was worth all the pain, all the anguish. I'd do it again if I had to, just for him." He rose to his feet, motioned with his hand toward the door, and smiled. "I want to meet him."

The two men walked into the den and stood looking through the sliding glass door. "There he comes now," Stephen said.

Jesus pulled the door aside. "Let's go meet him." Together they walked toward Saul of Tarsus.

# STRANGE MISSION

Juan del Monte sat up in bed with a start. What had he heard? Was he dreaming? No! There it came again. "Open up! This is the police!" A loud bang on the front door demanded action. Juan glanced over at his wife and saw her still asleep. Slipping from the bed, he put on his trousers. Then, closing the bedroom door behind him, he stumbled through the dark house to the front room.

"Is this some kind of trick?" he wondered. "Is some robber trying to get me to open the door? Or is it really the law? And what could the police want with me at this hour of the night?"

Opening the tiny window in the front door, Juan peered into the night. He could see the forms of two large policemen banging their billy clubs on the wooden door.

"What do you want?" Juan asked.

"Señor del Monte!" one of the policemen shouted.

"I am Señor del Monte," Juan replied as calmly as he could. "May I help you in any way?"

"Yes, you can open this door and let us in."

Unlocking the door, Juan swung it open. The two policemen, scowls on their faces, strode into his front room. "Where is your gun!" one of them demanded.

Juan felt the blood drain from his face. So that was it! Now he knew why they had come. He had recently bought a shotgun to protect his chickens from small animals. The law required that every citizen who owned a gun register it with the government by a certain date each year. Failure to do so meant spending a month in jail. Offenders suspected of plotting against the government received the worst treatment. But even the most well-behaved citizen who could prove that he merely forgot found himself locked up.

"I, I—I'll get it for you," Juan breathed. He put his hand to his mouth, then turned to go back to the bedroom where he kept the weapon. One of the policemen jerked Juan back by the shoulder. "You show me where that gun is, and *I'll* get it," he growled.

"My wife is in the bedroom, Señor." Juan bowed slightly. "I am not a bad man. I will not bring my gun out and shoot you. You may go in and get it. But may I explain to my wife first, and let her get dressed?" He gazed at the officer who had treated him so roughly. Their eyes met for a second as the man studied him.

"*Adelante* [Forward]!" he said. "Go! But leave the door open so we can hear."

Juan thanked the policeman and opened his bedroom door. "I'm in trouble," he said to Maria, his wife. "I forgot to register my gun with the authorities. The deadline was two weeks ago. Now they've come to get me. I'm afraid it will mean several weeks in prison. I understand that one month is the minimum sentence."

Maria buried her face in her pillow. "What will we do?" she wailed.

He patted her on the shoulder. "I know this is frightening, but I won't be in prison for anything bad. Just for an oversight. Who knows? Maybe God has a reason for allowing this. We must trust Him. In the morning you must get in touch with my boss and with Pastor Sucre. They may be able to help. Now dress quickly so the officers can come in and get the gun."

Opening the closet, Juan took out the gun. He placed it across a chair by the bed, then returned to the waiting policemen. "As soon as my wife is dressed, you may go in. The gun is on the chair."

A few minutes later a pale Maria emerged in her housecoat, a scarf around her hair. The officers' attitude seemed to soften when they saw her terrified expression.

"Pardon our intrusion, Señora," one of them said. "We are only doing what we were told to do."

"Sî, Señor."

"You may pick up the gun now if you wish," Juan told them, motioning toward the door with his hand.

One of the officers entered the bedroom and returned with the shotgun. "And now, Señor del Monte, you will come with us, please."

"Sí, Señor," Juan replied. "May I gather together a few things to take with me? I'm afraid I shall not be returning for a while."

Permission granted, Juan quickly finished dressing, then found a suitcase. Maria brought him a change of clothing, two sheets, and a blanket. On top of everything else, Juan laid his Bible and *Sabbath School Lesson Quarterly*.

"Take good care of the children while I'm gone," he said as he kissed Maria good-bye. "It won't be long till I'll be back."

At the police station Juan readily admitted having failed to register his gun. "It was an oversight," he explained to the interrogating officer. "I'm not a bad man. I have no wrong intentions against the government. As a Christian I believe in obeying the leaders of my country, not in shooting them down."

The officer appeared quite unimpressed as he shuffled through a stack of cards. Stopping at one, he grunted, adjusted his glasses, and examined it. "Señor Juan del Monte," he read aloud. "Offenses, none. Political record, clear." He paused. "I am authorized to give you the minimum of one month in prison if your record is clear. You will spend the night in a cell here at the police station. Tomorrow morning you will be transferred to the Bastión for a month."

The Bastión—that was the large, maximum-security prison at the edge of town. It housed some of the country's worst criminals. Of all places, it was the most feared. Juan wondered what awaited him

next as the guard led him through the door to the
cell in the back of the police station where he would
spend the night.

The rattle of a key in his door woke Juan early
the next morning. A friendly attendant handed him
a bowl of rice and beans. "You must eat quickly,
Señor," the attendant said. "One of the guards will
be here in a few minutes to take you to the Bastión."

"*Muchas gracias* [Thank you very much]." Taking the bowl, Juan wasted no time finishing his
breakfast. Then he sat on the edge of his cot and
picked up his Bible. He wanted a few minutes for
meditation and prayer before the guard came to get
him. "Lord," he said as he knelt to pray. "I don't
know why I'm here, but if there's some way I can
witness for You in this trial, if there's a work for me
to do during my month in prison, show me the
way."

At the Bastión two hours later an armed sentry
admitted Juan and his guard through a locked gate.
They entered a small waiting room where two other
prisoners sat, each with his personal guard. A
prison officer filled out papers at a desk at the far
end of the room. Juan and his guard took seats with
the others.

Half an hour later, his own paper work com-
pleted, Juan walked with his guard down a series of
long halls, through several locked and guarded
doors, to a section of the prison containing half a
dozen large, barred rooms. After a rattling of keys
and a banging of doors, Juan found himself in a
room with fourteen cots and about as many men.

Three cots lined the wall on either side of the door he had entered. Eight rested against the back wall, opposite the door. Beside each cot stood a small chest of drawers. At either end of the room a washbowl hung on the wall under a single cold-water faucet. In the center of the room, between the two rows of cots, stretched a long, narrow table.

After the guard left, Juan sat on the edge of his cot. The other men stared at him. Hard, bitter expressions marked most of their faces. Feeling conspicuous and a little uncomfortable, he remembered the stories he'd heard about prisoners who molested and beat up their fellow inmates.

"Father in heaven," he prayed silently, "I can only trust You to protect me. These men are the worst of sinners, but Jesus loved the worst of sinners and died for them. If I can help even one of them to learn to love You during the time I am here, it will be a month well spent. Help me to love them like You do."

As he prayed, the fear Juan had felt disappeared. "I must treat them like friends," he thought, and with a smile he held out his hand to the man nearest him. "My name is Juan del Monte."

At first the man just stared at him. "Pedro Alfonso," he mumbled at last and turned away. The rest of the men in the cell roared with laughter. Confused, Juan didn't know just what to say next, so he sat back down on the edge of his cot.

"Where are you from, Pedro?"

"From right here," the man replied wryly. The

other men laughed again.

"He means that he's been in this jail so long he doesn't know there's anyplace else to be from," one of them said in a derisive tone.

Juan realized that the men were laughing at Pedro, not at him. He felt sorry for the man and determined to get better acquainted with him. Reaching into his suitcase, he took out his Bible and quarterly. As he read he watched what went on around the room. Soon the other men were busy with their own conversations. Loud, coarse laughter told Juan he didn't care to hear some of the subjects under discussion. Pedro glanced his way.

"What do you do around here all day?" Juan asked him.

The cellmate shrugged. "Work out on the rock pile, only the guard is sick today, so we didn't have to go out."

"Must be pretty hard work," Juan commented, trying to keep the conversation going.

"You'll get used to it if you stay here as long as I have."

"They sent me here for a month because I forgot to register my gun," Juan explained.

"Lucky! I've been here almost ten years because I *used* mine, and I've got another ten to go. I was stupid. I got mad and killed a buddy while I was in the army. Then I tried to get away, and I killed a policeman, too. Stupid! Plain stupid! If I ever get out of here, I hope I can control my temper better."

"That's interesting," Juan replied. "One of my own hardest battles is with my temper. I thought I'd *never* conquer it, and I guess I really wouldn't have, either, but I met a Man who helps me. If I ask Him, He controls it for me."

"Yeah, I know. They tried to control mine in the army. They try to control it here too. It's nothing but force! force! force! all the time. I get so sick of it. Sometimes I go into a rage, like a madman. I could never make it on the outside. If I ever get out of here, I'll be right back. Nobody can control my temper, least of all me."

"I think the Person who helps me could help you too."

"What does he make you do?" Pedro asked bitterly.

"Just ask Him, that's all," Juan replied. "If you believe He can help you, He will."

"Humph! Nobody can help me."

"My Friend has always been able to help anyone who asked Him."

"What's his name?" Pedro questioned.

"Jesus."

For a long time Pedro sat thinking. "My mother was a Christian," he said at last. "She went to Mass every Sunday morning, and sometimes through the week too. But it never did her any good. I got my bad temper from her."

"Maybe she didn't know how to ask."

"Maybe not, maybe not." He sighed and looked the other way. Juan decided not to press the matter further just then. But he silently prayed for wisdom to know how he might lead Pedro to really know Christ.

The rest of that day Juan tried to get acquainted with the other prisoners. Some were friendly, others brushed him aside gruffly. The ones who spurned him seemed sad and discouraged. Feeling sorry for them, he wondered how he could help them to feel happier inside. He sensed that it was their sadness, the loneliness in their hearts, that had gotten many of them into trouble in the first place.

Before going to bed that night, Juan turned in his Bible to Matthew 25:35, 36. There he read, " 'For I was an . . . [hungered], and ye gave me meat: I was thirsty, and ye gave me drink: I was a stranger, and ye took me in: naked, and ye clothed me: . . . I was in prison, and ye came unto me.' "

"O God," Juan prayed quietly, "now I understand why You told us to visit the people in prison. They are lonely and discouraged. If we can just be friendly to them, let them know that someone cares, that may be all it takes to win some of them to You. Help me to live the way Jesus would if He were here. And especially help Pedro to understand how to ask You for help with his temper. Amen."

As Juan lay down to sleep that night he felt a peace he'd never known before. "And here I am in prison!" he chuckled. "I think I'm beginning to understand why I forgot to register my gun."

The next day the guard was sick again. "There must be a reason for it," Juan kept telling himself throughout the morning. "Maybe it was so Pedro couldn't go to work. How can I help Pedro?" He decided to leave his Bible and quarterly on the bed while he chatted with some of the dozen or so other prisoners in the cell. Noticing several men playing a game with homemade dominoes at the long table in the center of the room, he stood and watched. Eventually he fell into conversation with the man beside him and forgot about Pedro.

Half an hour later Juan chanced to glance toward his bed. He felt elated to see Pedro reading from the Bible he had left there. His first impulse was to speak to him, but he decided to give the Lord time to work through His Word. Perhaps, like the Ethiopian whom Philip met in the desert, Pedro would ask for an explanation. Juan kept up his conversation with the other prisoners in the circle around the domino game.

Another half hour passed. Juan strolled back to his bed and lay down to rest. Pedro continued reading. Although he had almost fallen asleep, Juan heard Pedro speak. "Did you say something?" he asked.

"Oh! I'm sorry. I should have asked for permission to read your Bible," Pedro explained. "After what you said yesterday, I decided to see if I could find out about the help Jesus gives with our bad tempers."

"The Word of God is free. You needn't apologize."

"But I don't think God wants me," Pedro sighed as he closed the Book and handed it back to Juan. "Some people who are good enough, yes. But not me. I'm too bad. God doesn't want anyone like me."

Juan thought a moment, then began, "Jesus told a story once. A farmer's son demanded of his father that he give him his share of the inheritance. Reluctantly the old man turned it over. But instead of spending his new wealth wisely, the boy squandered every penny of it on wild city living. When his money ran out, the young man had to tend a farmer's hogs."

"Just like me," Pedro muttered. "Only my father never gave me anything. He just threw me out of the house because I was such a rascal."

"This boy's father was different. The young man actually came to his senses one day, rather like you've done now. He decided to return to his father and just work as a hired servant. But his father would have none of it. He gave him the best clothes, threw a big party for him, and treated him exactly as before—like his son."

"Mine wouldn't do that!" Pedro glanced bitterly at Juan, then at the floor. "There's nobody would do a thing like that."

"God would."

"God? Huh! He kills sinners."

"Jesus came to tell us about God," Juan replied quietly. "In fact, this very story is one Jesus told to help us understand how God treats sinners who come to Him for help—kindly, like His own sons."

"I wish He would treat me like that," Pedro said.

"He already has." Juan turned to another text in the Bible. "It says right here that God loved the world so much—He loved sinners so much—that

He *gave* His only Son to die for us, and if we will just believe it, we can have eternal life."

"God kills sinners!" Pedro shot back. "That's what my mother always told me. Any time I did anything bad, she'd say, 'You'll go to hell if you don't straighten up. God will kill you for that!' "

"Maybe that's why your mother was never able to get God's help to overcome her bad temper," Juan suggested. "She probably never believed God loved her. Since she didn't believe He wanted to help her with her temper, she of course never asked for His help. I wouldn't ask somebody to help me, either, if I thought he hated me like that."

Pedro sat thinking for a long time. "I don't know," he said at last. "I just don't know. You sure are different. Nobody has ever explained it to me like this before. I must think about it."

"I will pray for you," Juan said quietly, "that God will help you to understand."

"Yes, pray for me, please."

Juan saw tears in Pedro's eyes as he turned away.

All the next week Juan and Pedro talked about God and His plan to save sinners from ruin and death. The dramatic change that came over Pedro's whole outlook on life amazed Juan. He had never fully realized the power the work of the Holy Spirit could have on a human heart. It showed not only in Pedro's attitude but on his face and in his language.

The sick guard stayed away only two days. After that, Pedro returned to work at the rock pile every morning. Juan's offense was minor, and the warden permitted him to stay in the cell all day. He missed talking with Pedro, but he spent each day preparing studies for him in the evenings. In just one week's time Juan covered every phase of the plan of salvation. And Pedro seemed eager to understand it all. Again, Juan recognized the Holy Spirit at work.

"*Amigo* [Friend], listen to this!" Pedro exclaimed one evening as he came in from the rock pile. "The guard yelled at me today like no one has ever done before. The devil really got after me. I was furious! I felt like exploding in the guard's face. Then I remembered God's promise to help us overcome if we ask Him. So I asked, and it worked! My anger left me. The guard looked so stunned that I almost laughed."

Juan felt he could explode right then, too, but for a different reason. "Isn't it wonderful what God can do for us!" he exclaimed. "Let's thank Him." Together they bowed their heads and prayed.

The morning of the ninth day in prison a guard came to the cell and unlocked the door. "Juan del Monte!" he barked.

Alone in the cell after the other prisoners left for the rock pile, Juan had lain down on his cot and fallen asleep. The guard's abrupt command jolted him. "Sî, Señor!" he replied, jumping to his feet. He smoothed his clothes with his hands as he stepped to the door.

"The warden wants to see you." The guard ushered Juan out the door and rattled the key in the lock. Together they passed through the same set of halls and doors Juan had passed through more than a week before. Juan entered the office ahead of the guard. An official behind the desk, whom Juan took to be the warden, motioned toward a chair. Wondering whether the news would be good or bad, Juan sat down.

"Señor del Monte," the warden began as he laid down a pencil and picked up a card. "I am happy to inform you that through the efforts of a Pastor Sucre, who has vouched for your integrity, we are permitting you to leave after ten days instead of four weeks."

Although Juan felt like jumping over the desk and hugging the man, he simply said, "Muchas gracias, Señor. I appreciate it very much."

"You will leave at about this same time tomorrow morning," the warden continued. "Señor Sucre will be here for you. That is all."

Juan glanced at the clock on the wall. It said ten o'clock. Thanking the warden again, he rose to leave the room. The guard ushered him out the door and back to his cell, where he spent most of the rest of the day planning for his final visit that evening with Pedro. Pedro still had much he must learn. They had covered the doctrines, to be sure. He could even find many of the texts in the Bible by himself. But he had not made a full commitment to accept everything, especially the Sabbath.

Juan wondered what would happen to Pedro after he left. He decided that the answer to that question would have to rest with the same God who had sent him here to find Pedro.

"I have news for you," Juan said as Pedro came over to his cot after work that evening.

"What is it? Good news or bad?"

Quietly Juan replied, "I will be released from prison at ten o'clock in the morning."

"Amigo, that is wonderful!" Pedro exclaimed. Then his tone became serious. "The Lord Jesus led you here. He knew that the time had come for this prodigal to return to his Father. Only the prodigal, like the lost coin, didn't know he had a loving Father to receive him as a son, so God sent you here to sweep out this prison to find me and show me the way back home."

Although there was a lump in his throat, Juan smiled. He didn't know what to say.

"I have some more questions," Pedro continued. "The Sabbath still troubles me. I think I understand that it's right, but how can I keep it? I'm not my own man here in this prison. The guards tell me what to do. How can I observe the Sabbath? It's impossible!"

Picking up his Bible, Juan turned to Mark 2:27, 28. "You see, Pedro," he explained, "it's not our choice whether to keep the Sabbath or not. Jesus Christ is Lord of the Sabbath. If He is Lord of our lives, too, then the Sabbath becomes an inseparable part of our experience with Him. It's not a question of whether or not the Sabbath is impossible to keep. For the Christian, that's settled. It's a question of whether we can truly be Christians if our Lord's Sabbath is not a vital part of our lives."

From Pedro's face Juan knew that the man

struggled with a great problem. Pedro's eyes fell to the floor where he stared at the concrete for a long time. Then he looked up at the light bulb in the ceiling. He glanced briefly at Juan, shifted his gaze back to the floor, then up to the ceiling again. Taking the Bible, he turned a few pages, but put it on the bed and walked to the wash basin against the wall for a drink. Returning, he sat on the edge of his cot.

"Look," he said. "I learned that God helps me overcome my temper. If I just keep quiet when the guard says something that makes me angry, everything works out like it should. Now you're telling me to talk back to that guard and make *him* mad! I mean, the Sabbath isn't his fault, you know. He's only doing what he's told to do. It's the warden and the government, all the way to the President of the country, that tell me what I have to do. I can't buck the system."

From the intensity on Pedro's face, Juan wondered if he would witness one of Pedro's temper tantrums right in the prison cell. The other prisoners seemed amused, but Juan brushed the thought of them out of his mind. He realized that Pedro's problem was not with doctrine. It involved his heart. Juan had explained the truth as clearly as he knew how. The rest he left up to the Holy Spirit.

"Pedro," he said, "I prayed that God would help you to understand His love and control your temper. Now I shall pray that God will help you with this Sabbath problem. Once you decide to follow Him all the way, He has an answer."

Juan felt that Pedro had entered the most critical moment of his life. A decision for eternity would take place that night, one way or the other. It seemed to Juan that if Pedro should leave for the rock pile the next morning without having reached a decision for Christ and the Sabbath, he might never make it. He determined to spend most of the night in prayer.

The study concluded, each man began preparing for the night. Juan turned back the blanket on his cot and set his Bible on a chair placed between their two cots. Pedro went to the basin for another drink. Back at his cot he took off his shoes and unbuttoned his shirt, hanging it over the back of the chair. He looked down at Juan's Bible, picked it up, and turned it over in his rough hands. "Mind if I study awhile from your Bible, amigo?"

"Not at all," Juan replied. "That's where the answers are, you know."

"Gracias." As he turned the pages he thought, "Answers! Don't I need them now!" Then his prayer winged heavenward. "God, it doesn't seem real. A week ago I was a criminal in my heart. Now You've changed all that. But that's *my* heart, not the guard's or the warden's. What am *I* supposed to do about *them*?"

Had Juan known the struggle that had raged in Pedro's heart since he had first learned of the Sabbath two days before, he would have understood a little better the reason for the sudden emotional outburst a few minutes earlier. To Pedro, the struggle was excruciating.

"It's one thing," he reasoned, "for Juan to tell me God will provide the answer. But it's something else for me to *believe* it when I know I'll have that guard and the warden and this whole prison down my throat the minute I refuse to work. And all the other prisoners. Won't they laugh when the guard makes a fool of me!"

Pedro spent an agonizing night. Tossing and turning, he thought of the guard, the warden, and the ridicule of the other prisoners. Then he thought of God's answer to his problem. Back and forth, around and around it went, all night long. Visions of the ten years that remained to his prison term stretching to twenty, then thirty, and forty for refusing to obey orders kept swirling through his mind. Finally he drifted off into a restless, fitful sleep.

He awoke early the next morning. Glancing over at Juan's bunk, he saw his friend kneeling in prayer. "He must be praying for me!" Pedro decided. Right then he knew what he must do. "If Jesus loved me enough to give His life for me," he thought, "then I must be willing to offer mine for Him. Thank You, Lord, for friends like Juan, who are willing to share their lives with others."

Breakfast was always a mad scramble as each man pushed and shoved to get his cup of food first. Pedro ate quickly, then took the opportunity to talk quietly with Juan before they parted for the last time.

"Amigo," he said, "I want you to know that I spent a most difficult night. I slept very little. The devil pulled one way, and God the other. But early this morning when I saw you praying for me, I made up my mind. Even if they kill me, I shall keep my first Sabbath day after tomorrow."

Juan grasped Pedro's hand. "That's wonderful!"

"*Atención!*" A guard's voice thundered in the prison cell. Every man except Pedro jumped into line in front of the cell door.

"If it's lifelong imprisonment, or even death, for refusing to obey orders, I shall obey God."

"Amigo, you must go now," Juan said, pointing to the men already filing out the door. "I shall be praying for you. God will answer our prayers." He reached down and picked up the Bible on his bed. "Here." He thrust it into Pedro's hands. "I can get another. You will need this one."

Pedro looked at the Bible he held in his hands. "Thank you, amigo. How can I thank you for everything!" He placed the Bible on his own cot and fell into line just as the last man walked out the door. The guard shot a scowl his way.

"I may get a lot more scowls before next Sabbath is over," Pedro mused as he broke into the sunshine outside. "But with a smile on my Father's face, what do I care? I'm His son, living in His home now."

Friday night Pedro sat on the edge of his cot thinking about the crisis he would face the next day. "If I refuse to leave this cell in the morning, I'll really catch it from the guard. Maybe I ought to go out to the rock pile and take my stand there. But if I do that, then I may weaken and lose the whole battle." Desperately Pedro wished he and Juan could talk things over and pray together again as they had every other evening that week. But then he remembered Juan's parting words: "God has the answer. I will be praying for you." He decided that he had trusted God to help him escape from a bad temper, and now he must rely on God for deliverance from this Sabbath problem.

Pedro rose early the next morning. He picked up the Bible Juan had left with him and studied God's promises. "Call upon me in the day of trouble," he read. "I will deliver thee, and thou shalt glorify me" (Psalm 50:15).

"Dear God," he prayed quietly, "I leave today and its events in Your hands. Give me the courage to take my stand in a way that will witness for You. Amen."

Breakfast over, Pedro knew it would be only a few minutes till the guard arrived to take them all to the rock pile. He still had not decided whether to insist on staying in the cell all day or whether to take his stand after reaching the rock pile.

"Atención!" The guard's command split the air. The men snapped to their feet and fell into line. Pedro's throat tightened. Now was no time to talk to the guard. But why talk? Just sit on the bed and wait for the worst to happen. He stepped to his cot.

"Adelante! March!" Pedro wavered. Glancing back at the door, his eyes met the guard's cold stare. He grabbed his Bible and quarterly and followed the last man out the door. The cell door slammed shut behind him. The time to choose where to take his stand had passed.

Pedro, in a daze, walked down the dimly lit gray hall. He scolded himself bitterly. "You coward! You just slipped along with the crowd. What will you do at the rock pile? Go along with the crowd again? Give in to the guard's command? God, help me to face the next test better."

Following the men through a heavy steel door, Pedro went from the dark building into the fresh air. Blinking in the bright light, he then took a deep breath and raised his head and chest high. Ahead of him the men walked single file past a stack of picks. Each man took one as he passed by. "Now is the time," Pedro thought. "I must not take a pick. It would be harder to refuse to work if I have a pick out there." He clutched his Bible and walked straight past the stack of tools. The guard failed to notice that he did not pick one up.

The pile of limestone where the men would spend the day lay just beyond a large tree, several hundred yards from the main building but still within the main prison compound. A narrow path wound to the left of the tree, dividing there to lead to the rock pile on the right and the guard's small hut on the left.

Slowly the line of men twisted along the path toward the stack of limestone. Pedro's heart pounded as they neared the tree, and beads of perspiration formed on his forehead. Taking another deep breath, he pulled in his stomach to calm the tension under his belt. Just as he reached the tree, the guard forced his way past, pushing Pedro roughly aside on his way to the front of the line. Pedro stumbled over to the tree where he sat down between two large roots and laid his Bible on the ground.

The guard barked several orders and retreated to his hut. Propping his rifle against the outside wall, he slumped down on the chair. Several minutes passed. To Pedro, each minute seemed an hour. He forced another breath of air against the fluttering in his stomach. Surveying the group of men around the rock pile, he noticed that nobody there had missed him either—yet. His taut muscles began to relax. He leaned against the tree, closed his eyes, and relaxed some more. "Maybe it won't be so bad after all," he thought. Several more minutes passed. Nothing happened.

Pedro had relaxed almost completely and was about to pick up his Bible when a shriek split the air. "Who escaped?"

He jerked his head toward the hut. A chill shot through his arms and legs as he saw the guard grab his gun and leap toward the startled prisoners. Terrified, he clutched the roots of the tree.

"Stay where you are, every man of you!" the guard screamed. "I counted, and one man's gone. I'm responsible. Who got away?" His shout rose to a terrifying pitch. The bewildered men crouched under the guard's tirade. The guard whirled this way and that, searching desperately for the missing man. Horrified at what might happen next, Pedro clamped his eyes shut.

"Pedro Alfonso! You worthless, good-for-nothing scoundrel!" the guard screamed. Then followed a tirade of oaths as the guard's boots beat a path toward the tree.

There rose in Pedro's heart the same anger that had gripped him every other time when the guard tore into him with his tongue. Rage pounded in his mind. "Force! force! nothing but force, force, force, all my life! Why can't I keep the Sabbath the way I want to!" he thought. "Who's he to tell me I . . ." Suddenly Pedro recognized the demon that had intruded into his mind. He recognized the rage, the madness, that God had helped him to overcome only a few days before.

"God, help me to control my temper before this enraged man!" he prayed. Like an escape valve opening in his heart, the pressure vanished. His hands relaxed. No longer did he feel angry at the guard. No longer did he fear what might happen because of his refusal to work. The Bible text flashed across his mind again, "Call upon me in the day of trouble: I will deliver thee, and thou shalt glorify me."

The enraged guard hurled his rifle to the ground and grabbed Pedro by the collar of his prison uniform. "Get to work, you wretched worm!"

Pedro felt himself flying toward the pile of rocks. Picking himself up from the dust, he turned around and faced his tormentor again.

"Look, I said work!" the guard screamed. He stamped a frenzied pattern on the ground. "Isn't it enough that you scared me half out of my skin?

Work, I say, *work!* Where's your pick?"

"I don't have a pick," Pedro replied quietly.

"You don't have a pick? You walked past the stack like all the rest. Were your hands numb? or just your head?"

Pedro heard a ripple of laughter from the men as he explained, "I passed the pile like the rest, but I did not take one because God does not want me to."

The guard's jaw fell, and for a moment he just stared at Pedro. "This is ridiculous!" he exploded. "First you scare the life out of me, and now you try to tell me about some vision from God."

"No," Pedro said calmly, "I have not had any vision from God. I have been reading from His Word, and in the Bible it says that Saturday is the Sabbath, God's holy day. That is the day He has commanded us to rest, and I must obey Him."

"I never read anything like that in the Bible," the guard retorted. "And what difference if I had? This is prison, not church. You obey me, not God."

"I am sorry, but my Bible tells me that God's commands come before man's. I can show you if you wish."

"You what?"

"In my Bible, right over there." Pedro pointed to the Book under the tree.

The guard whirled and looked at the Bible, then turned back to the prisoner. "Come with me," he ordered. Taking Pedro by the arm, he dragged him under the shade of the tree.

"Back to work!" he shouted with a wave of his hand toward the other prisoners who still stood by the rock pile. The men squatted on the ground and took up their rocks and picks. "Now this I must see," he said to Pedro. "Where?"

"In God's Ten Commandments, right here. 'Remember the sabbath day, to keep it holy.' " Pedro read the entire commandment, then explained it to the guard.

"Man, what's happened to you these past few days?" the guard demanded.

"What do you mean?"

"I mean you're different. A week ago you scorched my eardrums with your anger, but today I practically blast you from the face of the earth, and you stand here calmly talking to me about God." The guard waved both arms in the air. "What's gotten into you?"

"Do you remember Juan?" Pedro asked.

"You mean the man who forgot to register his gun? The one whose preacher got him out of here two days ago?"

"Yes, him."

"What about him?"

"He told me about Jesus and how He helps people to overcome their bad tempers. I tried it, and it works. Jesus helps me to control my tongue so that I'm no longer angry. And I figure that if the God of the Bible, who can control my tongue, tells me to keep the Sabbath, that must be important, too. That's why I cannot work today."

The guard turned around and beckoned to the men at the rock pile. "*Hombres* [Men], come here. Listen to this man preach. You need it!"

The men needed no second invitation to leave their work under the scorching sun and sit in the shade of a tree. Throwing down their picks, they scrambled to where Pedro and the guard stood and sat in a circle around them.

"Amigos," the guard said, "you may not like sermons, but they are better than work on a hot day like this. Listen to what this man says." The guard walked over to his rifle, sat down, and laid it across his legs as he faced Pedro. All that morning and through the afternoon Pedro talked to the men about his newfound faith. Some of them became bored and slept, but others listened. On some faces Pedro saw genuine concern for the kind of lives they had been living.

For several weeks the guard permitted Pedro to speak to the convicts on Sabbath instead of their working. After a time Pedro received permission to spend the Sabbath in his cell.

One morning several months later Pedro started to follow the other prisoners out the door to work when the guard stopped him. "Amigo," he called, "you aren't supposed to go to work today. The warden wants to see you. Another guard will come for you when he is ready."

Pedro was stunned. Had his Sabbathkeeping gotten him into trouble after all? Shaken, he returned to the cell as the door slammed shut behind him. "Dear God," he prayed aloud as he picked up his Bible. "I don't know what this is all about. But You helped me through the last test, and I trust You to help me through this one too. If it means ten more years in prison, I've learned that I'm far more free in prison with You than I could ever be on the outside without You. Help my faith to remain strong."

Two hours later, Bible in hand, Pedro accompanied a guard through the same halls and steel doors that his friend Juan had passed through some months before. Reaching the warden's office, the guard opened the door and stepped inside. Pedro followed him and stood before a group of five men, the warden in the center.

"Sit down," the warden said. He motioned to a chair in front of his desk. Pedro did, laying his Bible in his lap. "This group of men," the warden began—in a tone of voice that Pedro found difficult to interpret— "has been reviewing your case, Señor Alfonso." Had they decided to stop his Sabbath privileges? he wondered. His hands gripped the Bible a little tighter.

"We know, of course, of the incident at the rock pile several months ago," the warden continued. "We also know of your talks with the men on Saturdays for several weeks after that."

Now Pedro felt sure they would take his Sabbath privilege away. "Help me to remain faithful, whatever the cost," he prayed silently.

"In speaking with the guards and the other prison personnel who have come in contact with you," the warden continued, "we feel that a genuine change has taken place in your life. Pastor Sucre has met with this parole board and has assured us that should you be released from prison, he is willing to assist you in making the adjustment to life on the outside. The board feels that a man who has changed as much as you have ought not to remain in prison any longer. Therefore, as of this day, you are a free man."

Pedro bowed his head and buried his face in his hands. His frame shook with emotion.

The warden opened the door behind his desk. Into the room stepped Juan and Pastor Sucre. They walked over to where Pedro, face still buried in his hands, wept quietly in his chair. Juan put his hand on Pedro's shoulder. "Amigo."

Pedro looked up. "Juan!" he gasped, jumping to his feet. The two men put their arms about each other's shoulders.

A few minutes later they walked out of the prison with Pedro's things in a suitcase. "Thank You, Lord," Juan breathed, "for letting me forget to register my gun so I could enter this prison and set another of Satan's prisoners free!"

## GIVE US THIS DAY

Twenty-five children crowded the small school building in old England. Miss Mabel Murphy, the teacher, sat behind her desk, her back straight, her hair pulled to a tight bun on top of her head. She glanced at the clock ticking on the shelf in the back of the room. Her heavy skirt swept the floor as she walked around to the front of her desk.

"Children!"

They straightened up on their benches and held their slates in their laps. Two boys sharing the same bench poked at each other.

"Boys! We'll have no more of that!" Swallowing their grins, they put their hands in their laps.

"It's almost time to go home," Miss Murphy announced. "Helen, would you please see that the smaller ones have their coats on before they leave?"

A tall girl wearing a faded blue dress stood. Her long black hair, parted down the middle and framing her thin face and tired eyes, reached to her waist. She moved to the back of the room with a firm step, gathered up half a dozen small wraps from pegs on the wall, and took them one by one to

70

the youngest children. A little boy touched her hand as she passed by. Smiling, she patted him on the head and returned to her place.

"Now everyone stand, and we will repeat the Lord's Prayer together," Miss Murphy requested.

The children shuffled on their benches, braced themselves against the long boards that made the desk tops, and rose to their feet

"Bow your heads."

The children lowered their faces and closed their eyes. Several of the smaller ones folded their hands.

"Our Father which art in heaven . . ."—a chorus of voices repeated the prayer in unison with Miss Murphy— "Hallowed be thy name. Thy kingdom come. Thy will be done in earth, as it is in heaven. Give us this day our daily bread. . ."

Helen glanced at Miss Murphy, then quickly lowered her head again and shut her eyes during the rest of the prayer. Miss Murphy dismissed the children and returned to her desk. She didn't notice Helen waiting nearby until the girl coughed slightly. "Oh, yes, Helen, what can I do for you?"

Helen approached and rested her hands on Miss Murphy's desk. "Miss Murphy, I wanted to ask you about the Lord's Prayer."

"Yes, dear, what is it you don't understand?"

"Well, where it says, 'Give us this day our daily bread,' what does that mean?"

"That, my child, is a request our Lord told us to make of our Father, who will provide for all our needs."

"But what if He doesn't?"

The teacher smiled and touched Helen's hands. She looked into her eyes and paused before she spoke. "God always provides," she said in a gentle voice. "Sometimes He tests our faith, but His promises are sure."

After a deep breath Helen thanked Miss Murphy and left the room.

A thick hedge ran along one side of the path that led from the school to the small village nearby. A low rock wall beside a row of oak trees marked the edge of the field on the other side of the path. Birds, building their nests, chirped in the trees. Helen stayed in the warm sunshine as much as possible as she walked toward home. She passed by several farmers' homes, small stone cottages with thatched roofs, surrounded by spring flowers and vegetable gardens.

At a bend in the road she paused and gazed across the fields that sloped to a low cliff at the far end. Beyond the cliff lay the sea. The girl sniffed the salt air and searched the distant horizon for several minutes. She seemed scarcely to notice a farmer in the field, guiding a plow behind his horse, or a dog that barked at a cat beside the cottage nearby or two honeybees that buzzed past.

Helen's father, Elias Foster, was a sea captain. He had left home on a voyage six months before, saying he would be home by the middle of March. But now it was nearly June, and still he had not returned or sent word with any other returning vessel about a change in his plans. Her mother, Martha Foster, had been especially quiet about the house the past couple of weeks. With five children to feed, and one of them a baby less than a year old, Helen understood why.

She sighed and bent her steps once more toward home. Soon she walked down a narrow, winding street. The whitewashed buildings, huddled against each other, opened directly onto the street on one side and onto a narrow sidewalk on the other.

The girl heard a clatter of hooves and loud shouts around the bend in the street ahead. She gulped and pressed into a doorway. Two horses, then four, galloped into view, followed by a gold and purple carriage with lavish carvings on the front and sides and topped with silver ornaments.

"Hi! Ho! Hi! Ho!" bellowed the muscular driver on the seat at the top. He waved a whip high in the air and cracked it over the horses' backs. The spirited animals raised their heads, whinnied, and clattered on down the street.

Her heart still pounding, Helen pulled away from the door and continued down the street, more briskly now. She knew that the carriage belonged to the king, who had a summer palace in the country nearby. Many of the townsfolk worked on the royal estate, and they had been especially busy of late. Rumor had it that in a few days the king and queen would arrive from London for their first visit of the season.

Farther on, the street widened and the buildings were set back, with gardens and flowers around them. A few minutes later Helen found her mother, with the baby on one hip, visiting in their garden with Mrs. Benton, a neighbor. She could hear her two younger brothers and her sister playing tag behind the house.

"But, Martha, my dear, don't you worry?" Mrs. Benton asked.

"It's hard, not knowing where he is or why he doesn't return," Mrs. Foster replied. "But I trust God to take care of him."

Mrs. Benton hesitated before she spoke again. "How are you doing for food?" she asked.

Helen noticed that her mother caught her breath before she replied. Then she smiled. "We'll be all right. The garden will be coming on soon, you know."

The neighbor glanced at the neat rows of plants in front of the house and to the side. "Yes, I suppose so. That will help a lot, when things begin to come on." She looked back at Mrs. Foster. "Well, I must be going now. Things are pretty busy in the kitchen at the palace, and if I don't hurry, I'll be late for work."

The girl followed her mother into the house and sat on a bench beside the large oak table in the main room. The house seemed dark in contrast to the bright sunshine outside. Her gaze darted over to the flour barrel in the corner, the ladles and mixing spoons hanging on the wall, and the low fire burning in the hearth. Thinking she heard her mother say something, she turned toward her, only to see her still holding the baby, her hand over her forehead, leaning with her head bowed against the doorway into the bedroom. Even in the dim light Helen could see the lines in her mother's face.

"Mamma," she called. She waited for her mother to reply. "Mamma." Still no answer. Helen walked over and lightly touched her mother on the sleeve of her dress.

"Oh!" her mother gasped. "Did you say something?"

"Mother, you *are* worried."

"I do worry about your father and whether he's safe," Mrs. Foster told her.

"And about whether we'll have enough to eat?" Helen asked.

Helen's mother smoothed back the baby's hair several times with her hand. Then she turned to Helen. "I'm sure he'll be back soon. Why don't you go out and hoe the weeds in the garden so that it will look nice when he comes? Get the other children to help you. I'll be out when I get the baby to sleep."

Each day after school Helen searched the sea for some sign of her father's arrival. She hoped she would find him in the house when she got home. But she half knew he wouldn't be there, and he wasn't. Her mother seemed more and more preoccupied as time went by.

Her younger brothers and sisters were playing in the garden as usual when Helen returned home one day about a week later, but she sensed something was wrong the minute she stepped inside the house. It seemed strangely silent. Helen blinked in the dark and made her way to the bedroom. She found her mother sitting on the edge of the bed, weeping. "Mamma," she cried, "is there bad news? Has something happened to Father?"

Mrs. Foster shook her head and pressed her handkerchief to her eyes. Helen sat down beside her on the bed. She felt her mother slip her arm around her and draw her close. The girl could see her bloodshot eyes, and her eyelids, red around the edges and swollen, looked as though she had been crying a long time. "No," Mrs. Foster said at last, "there is no news from your father. That's the trouble."

Helen drew away from her mother and looked straight into her face. "Mamma," she said, "is it because there is no more food in the house?"

"There is still food. Go get the other children."

The girl went to the door and called her brothers and her sister from their play. They came skipping and laughing, but the laughter faded the moment they stepped across the threshold into the house. As if afraid of disturbing someone who was sick or in a deep sleep, they tiptoed about the room.

"Sit down at the table," Helen whispered.

The children moved quietly to their places on either side of the table. Helen joined them. A moment later Mrs. Foster entered the room and took a pan from the shelf. She set it on the table and removed a white cloth that covered it. Five brown buns lay in the bottom.

"Let us thank God in heaven for the food He has graciously provided," Mrs. Foster said. "When I am through praying, we will all repeat the Lord's

Prayer together."

The children bowed their heads and folded their hands.

"Dear God," Mrs. Foster began, "we thank Thee for providing for our needs. We acknowledge Thy blessing in placing this bread on the table to satisfy our hunger and nourish our bodies. Help us to glorify Thy name with all our strength." She glanced at the children before she spoke again: "Our Father which art in heaven. . . ."

The children joined in the prayer: "Hallowed be thy name. Thy kingdom come. Thy will be done in earth, as it is in heaven. Give us this day our daily bread. . . ."

Opening her eyes Helen watched her mother. Mrs. Foster bit her lip before she continued. "And forgive us our debts, as we forgive our debtors," she said at last. "And lead us not into temptation, but deliver us from evil: For thine is the kingdom, and the power, and the glory, for ever. Amen."

Their mother opened her eyes after the family had finished. "Children, I must tell you something."

Helen noticed that her mother's voice trembled. She saw her bite her lower lip and twist a handkerchief between her hands. The younger children gazed silently at their mother.

"My dears, Father has not come home, and the flour barrel is empty." She nodded toward it in the corner. "I made these buns from the last of our flour this morning. They will carry us through the night. I do not know what we will do for food tomorrow.

I'm afraid that . . ." Her voice choked, and she didn't finish the sentence.

"Mamma," Helen said, looking at her mother, "we just got through praying, 'Give us this day our daily bread.' God will provide food for us tomorrow, and we don't have to worry about it."

Mrs. Foster rested her forehead on her hand a few seconds. "Thank you, my dear," she whispered. "Forgive my lack of faith." She picked up the pan of buns and passed them around the table.

Each child took one and held it between his hands. The children seemed to hover about the table with wide eyes. Mrs. Foster took the last bun. They ate silently, almost as though they were observing a religious ritual.

Helen was just ready to put the last bite of her bun in her mouth when she heard a gentle knock at the door. "I'll get it," she said. When she opened the door, Mrs. Benton entered, carrying a large basket in her arms.

"I hope you don't mind," Mrs. Benton told her, setting the basket on the table. "The king and queen didn't come to the palace yesterday as planned, so all the food prepared for the ball last night will go to waste unless we can find someone who can use it."

The children gathered about the basket and stared. Mrs. Foster came to Mrs. Benton's side and slipped an arm around her waist. "Thank you, my dear," she whispered. "It certainly will help."

"Good!" Mrs. Benton said. "And there's plenty more where this came from if you can use it. Send the boys down to the palace kitchen in a few minutes, and I'll see that they get all they can carry. Helen can come too. And now I must get back."

The neighbor left. The children jumped up and down and clapped their hands. "God did provide, Mamma!" one of the boys exclaimed. "He gave us enough bread for many days."

Helen and her mother looked at each other and smiled. The girl noticed that her mother's eyes sparkled. "God did provide," Mrs. Foster repeated. "And from the king's own table!"

# REVENGE

Elijah swept his arm in a wide arc toward the slaves bending over the cotton field in the boiling afternoon sun. "Dey nebber finish pickin' de field tonight, Massa," he said.

"They did a field larger than this in a day's time last week," Ichabod Kurston growled. "Why can't they do this one?"

"But las' week coola, Massa. Dey's not like machines, what don' mind de sun." His brown eyes gazed steadily into Ichabod's face.

"Come!" Kurston ordered.

Elijah followed his master to a thatched canopy at the edge of the field. He ducked as he stepped under the shelter.

From the low hilltop where they stood, Kurston surveyed the fields of the plantation that stretched in the distance on every side. "And how," he demanded, "are we going to get all those fields harvested before the rains come if those lazy slaves can't move in a little heat?" He squared his shoulders and scowled at Elijah.

"But Massa buy de small plantation to de south

las' winter," Elijah replied. "De slabes dat do de work las' yeah canna' do all dat too, dis yeah. Massa mus' buy more slabes."

Ichabod spat on the ground. "How many?" he snapped.

"Massa need at leas' twenny more slabes."

"Twenty more mouths to feed!" Kurston muttered. "Might as well not have bought the Jeremiah Williams place." He looked up at Elijah. "OK, we'll go into town tomorrow and get them. I want you along."

"Yes, Massa."

Just then a young girl emerged from the fields, dragging a bag of cotton behind her. She struggled in front of the shelter toward a wagon standing nearby. Elijah sprang to her side. "Elijah hep you wi' dat cotton."

The girl smiled. Picking up her sack, Elijah dumped the load into the wagon with the rest of the cotton.

Once again Ichabod spat on the ground, then walked toward the plantation stables.

Elijah had been born in Africa. He had already reached manhood when a group of slave drivers, led by a stubby African native, marched into his village one day. The African helped them snatch up all the able-bodied young men and haul them in chains to the ships.

The faces of the white slave traders soon faded from Elijah's mind, but he never forgot the cruel African who grew wealthy from the bodies of his own people. Resentment against the man burned in

Elijah's heart. The fact that in America he could never gain revenge fanned the bitterness into a passionate hate.

At first Elijah avenged his wrath on his new master, a short man who in spite of the color of his skin reminded him of his enemy. Slouching around the plantation, he arrived at work late and did no more than he absolutely had to. He snarled and glared and threatened every time Kurston got after him. Elijah did everything in his power short of open rebellion to oppose his master. Kurston almost never ventured out alone after dark, and Elijah sensed that it was because his master secretly feared him.

But in time Elijah came under the influence of Christian slaves who taught him to love his enemies. Gradually a change came over him. He pitied the weaker slaves, especially the young and the elderly. And he learned to respect his master, who over the years entrusted more and more of the management of the estate to his care. The slave still retained a sense of superiority over the white man, but he felt a certain pride with his master for the success of the plantation.

In the market the next day, Kurston strode up and down the line of slaves with Ahab, the slave dealer. "Elijah, I want you to choose slaves you can manage, strong men who can work hard."

A moment later Elijah motioned to a tall, rugged black man with muscular arms. When the Negro stepped from the line, Ahab grunted, "Seventy-five dollars."

Elijah chose a slave with a pitted face, another with smooth, lean muscles, and a youngster barely into his teens but who stood tall and strong already. Ahab called off the price of each one.

Moving down the line, Elijah came upon an old man, thin and slightly bent. He stopped and studied him carefully. The aging slave shuffled, fixing his eyes on the ground. For a second Elijah started to move on, then he suddenly turned around and motioned the old man out of the line.

"Not him!" Kurston growled.

Elijah turned to his master. "Massa tell me to choose who I want."

"But he can't even earn his own food."

"I want dat black man."

Ahab stepped forward. "Since you're buying twenty slaves, I'll let you have the old man for nothing," he volunteered.

Kurston grunted. "I guess you will, to get him off *your* hands." He nodded to Elijah. "Get going."

Fifteen minutes later the slave driver handed Kurston a paper with the names of twenty-one slaves written in bold, black letters. Kurston took it and scanned it a moment, then reached for the pen that Ahab held out. "I. Kurston," he scrawled with a flourish at the bottom.

He watched Elijah talk to the slaves on the way home, especially to the old man, Simeon. "Look," Ichabod said to Elijah when they reached the plantation. "It's enough that I bought the wretch. I don't want you wasting all your time on him. If he can't produce, let him alone."

Elijah said nothing. Later Kurston watched him
show the new slaves to their quarters. He noticed
that Elijah took Simeon to his own cabin and spent
several extra minutes making him comfortable. Just
then the plantation owner's wife called him to din-
ner. Ichabod spat on the ground and walked inside.
"Sentimental slave," he muttered as he sat down to
the table.

"I think Elijah's very kind," his wife protested
after he explained what he meant. "He certainly has
changed in the past few years."

"It's a good thing he's learned to be so reponsi-
ble about the place," Kurston muttered, "or I
wouldn't have him. I never saw anyone make such
a fuss over a creature as he's doing over that Simeon. The old man's as useful as an antique."

Every spare minute Elijah spent caring for Simeon. Scouring the place for scrap lumber, he built
him a bunk in his own hut. He sewed together a
cotton pad that was better than anything any of the
other slaves had to sleep on. Kurston noticed that
Simeon went about in some of Elijah's own clothes,
and nights he could see Elijah sewing garments by
the dim light of a candle in his hut. At the evening
meals Elijah always saw that Simeon received the
best of everything, even if it meant that he himself
had to do with a little less.

It all seemed a bit silly to Kurston till one day
Elijah showed up late for work. But he picked cotton that day like Kurston had never seen a slave do
before. Sometimes he brought in a bag an hour.
When he wasn't picking cotton, he was helping

other slaves drag theirs in to weigh it and organizing them to pick the fields more efficiently. Once he even helped the water boy pass water around, and always he spoke encouraging words that seemed to make all the slaves move faster.

On the third day Kurston noticed that Elijah labored harder than ever, and he seemed to have a subdued attitude about him. He still spoke encouragingly to the other slaves, but his voice seemed more quiet and more urgent. "Is it because he's afraid the rains will overtake us?" Kurston wondered. The plantation owner knew that already the rains were overdue a week, and still a week's work remained to get in all the cotton. But Elijah quit work early that evening and went to his hut.

The next morning he showed up even later than before. Still Kurston said nothing. But when he looked for Elijah at noon and someone told him that he had gone to his hut, he decided that he had to do something. He stalked off in the direction of the slave quarters.

Entering the dark hut from the bright sunshine, Kurston could scarcely see. "Elijah!" he called.

"Yes, Massa, I be here."

Ichabod peered in the direction from which the voice came. In the dim light he could barely make out the dark form of Elijah kneeling on the floor beside a bunk. Simeon lay on it, moaning.

"Elijah! What does this mean?" Ichabod demanded. "You're supposed to be working in the fields."

"Yes, Massa, but Simeon, he a very sick slabe."

By now Ichabod's eyes had adjusted to the dark. He could see Elijah sponging the old man's forehead with a damp cloth. "Simeon isn't a slave," Kurston retorted. "I told you not to get him."

"But, Massa, he a man, a sick man what needs my help. I be out in de fields again soon as I cool his face."

Anger flashed in Kurston's eyes. "Who is this slave, anyway?" he demanded. "Why are you so anxious to take care of him? Is he your father?"

"No, Massa, he not be my fader."

"Then he must be your brother or your uncle."

"No, Massa, he not my brudda, and he not my uncle."

"He's a friend, then?"

"No, Massa, he not my friend. Simeon be my enemy."

"Your what?"

"Yes, Massa, he my enemy, an' de Lawd Jesus, He say to lub our enemies an' do dem good." Elijah paused. "Dis Simeon, he be de man what sol' me to de slabe traders many yeahs ago when I a free man in my village in Africa. Now I finds him an' does him good, like de Good Book say."

Ichabod's face paled. He stammered and choked and stumbled out of the hut into the light.

# THE FOOL'S PRAYER

*Friday, December 30*

Karl Kroulik entered Heilmann's office and snapped a salute. The commandant looked up and motioned toward a chair. "Sit down," he growled.

Kroulik's high black boots rapped the floor. He crossed the room and sat down.

Heilmann lowered his eyebrows. "And what did you find out from Patzke?"

"He's adamant, sir. Says he can't work tomorrow. Nothing changes his mind."

"Lazy, good-for-nothing prisoner," Heilmann muttered. He pushed aside a black, cone-shaped paperweight from a stack of papers on his desk. Picking up a document from the top, he leaned back in his swivel chair and studied the paper.

Adolph Heilmann, in his steel-gray uniform, was a large man—not so tall but massive about the chest and shoulders. A jagged scar ran down his left cheek and under his heavy square jaw. He had dark eyes, and a dark look about them, under dark, bushy eyebrows, and the hard scowl on his face never left any doubt about who was in command.

His fingers, short and solid, were set on a thick palm that could clench a huge, iron fist.

Taller, with blond hair—rather a dirty blond— Kroulik had a cold, even stare to his blue eyes that told you he was looking at you intently but never revealed what he thought.

The commandant replaced the document under the black marble paperweight and glanced at Kroulik. "Let him off work like he wants!" he snapped.

Kroulik jolted upright in his chair.

Heilmann's forehead drew to a frown, but his mouth smiled. "Yes, let him off," he repeated. Then he half stood and shook a finger at Kroulik. "But tell him he works all night Saturday and all day Sunday—twenty-four hours straight without a break!" He settled back in his chair and folded his arms. "Give him a *nice* outside job. In this freezing weather and with the kind of food our good cooks prepare for these people, I think before long Patzke won't be asking for time off anymore."

"You might be interested in something Patzke said, sir," Kroulik interrupted, his eyebrows narrowing.

"What was that?"

"The window was ajar as I approached the barracks to see him this morning, and I heard his voice; so I stopped to listen. You never know what valuable information may turn up like that."

Heilmann nodded.

"I must have arrived at the end of the conversation because all I heard was, 'And deliver me from this trial in a way that will glorify Thy name and witness for Thee. Amen.' "

"The fool!" Heilmann muttered.

*Friday, January 27*

Heilmann burst into his office ahead of a cold blast of air. He jerked off his overcoat and threw it over a chair. Chunks of snow broke from the heavy wool and dropped to the floor. The telephone rang just as he sat down.

"Yes?" He paused. "I should say I have time for that!" He replaced the receiver on the telephone and began sorting through the papers that lay scattered about his desk. Five minutes later the door opened, and Kroulik stepped into the office and saluted.

"Sit down," Heilmann growled. "Tell me about Patzke. Any progress?"

"I spoke to the cook, sir," Kroulik reported, "and he's cooperating. I've given Patzke the heaviest outside work I could find. He shows signs of tiredness most of the time."

Heilmann rubbed his chin between the thumb and forefingers of his left hand. "It won't be long now. Next time you report to me, have the camp doctor examine him first and tell us what kind of progress we're making. That is all." After Kroulik strode out the door, Heilmann returned to **his** work.

*Friday, February 24*

Kroulik knocked at the door and listened. A

gruff voice answered from the other side. "Enter!"

Heilmann stood behind the desk, his arms folded, his eyes lowered. "Yes?"

"I came to see you about Patzke, sir."

The commandant raised his eyebrows and nodded. "Ah-h, yes! Sit down." Kroulik waited till his superior sat down, then took a chair. "Well, has he changed his mind yet?" Heilmann asked.

Drawing a yellow paper from his inside coat pocket, Kroulik handed it to him. "Patient is undernourished," Heilmann read, "underweight, and shows signs of extreme exhaustion." He glanced at Kroulik. "Good work. And what's the program doing to the patient's head?"

Kroulik eyed Heilmann coldly. "Nothing, sir."

Heilmann frowned and his mouth stretched to a tight, white line. For a minute he sat in thought, then turned to Kroulik. "Keep it up! He'll give. It won't be long now." He picked up the tall, cone-shaped paperweight from his desk, removed a document, and signed it.


*Friday, March 31*

"What is it?" Heilmann snapped when he glanced up as Kroulik entered his office.

"Patzke."

"Yes! Sit down." Heilmann glowered at Kroulik. "How are things going? Any improvement?"

"Yes and no," Kroulik muttered. "Patzke's so sick he can hardly get out of bed. The past two days I haven't been able to get him as far as the door."

"Good! Excellent!" Heilmann slapped his knee and twirled half a turn in his chair.

Lowering his head, Kroulik eyed the commandant from under his eyebrows. "Except for one *thing*."

Jerking back around in his chair, the commandant glared at him. Kroulik nodded. The room took on a funereal silence. Heilmann's jaw tightened, and fire shot from his eyes. His voice came low, tense, and even. "Tell Patzke," he snarled—and he spoke each word slowly, deliberately—"tell Patzke that tomorrow morning he works or he *dies*. If exhaustion won't change his mind, maybe a firing squad will. That is all."

*Saturday, April 1*

*8:00 AM.* Heilmann's office door flew open. The commandant stormed to his desk and snatched the receiver from the phone. Dialing three numbers, he waited. A moment later his eyes narrowed to slits, and he spat into the phone, "Kroulik, I want to see you the minute you're through with Patzke." He threw the receiver back on the hook.

The commandant's eyes darted about the desk from paper to document to prison record. The telephone rang. He answered it. Two guards called. He dispatched them. He dashed off a letter, read through a report, then shoved everything into a pile in one corner of the desk. A knock came at the door.

"And what's the situation this morning?" Heilmann demanded as Kroulik entered.

"The mind or the body?"

"Both."

"He's too sick to work," Kroulik hissed. He paused and tightened his lips. "And he wouldn't if he could."

Heilmann's eyes blazed. The veins in his neck bulged. Crimson tinted the edge of his collar, crept to his ears, and spread across his face to his brow. Standing, he leaned toward Kroulik and slammed a fist on the desk.

"The fool!" he roared. "He dies!" Settling back in his chair, Heilmann lowered his eyes. His voice quiet and steady, every word measured, he said, "Call every prisoner in this camp out to the drill field. Line up the firing squad, and be sure they have real bullets in their guns. This is no bluff." His voice rose. "Tell the prisoners this is what we do to the man who dares to disobey orders." Leaning over the desk, he shrieked, "Then get Patzke. Tie his hands behind his back and force him to walk to the field. I don't *care* how sick he is!" Heilmann doubled his fist and shook it at Kroulik. "Shoot the idiot," he screamed. "Shoot him so everyone can see what happens to the man who thinks his God can deliver him!" He fell back into his chair.

*10:00 AM*. Kroulik hurried into the commandant's office, his face the color and the look of a ghost. His eyes were drawn and haggard as he slumped to Heilmann's desk.

"Well?"

"I did as you said, sir. The prisoners are all on the field. The firing squad is ready." Kroulik gasped for breath.

"What did you tell the prisoners?"

"I told them they were going to see what happens to fools who disobey orders."

"And then?" Heilmann glared at him.

"I went to get Patzke."

"And then?" The commandant clutched the paperweight.

"I ordered him from his bunk."

"And then?"

"I tore off his blanket and jerked him from the bed."

Heilmann's purple face exploded with rage. His eyes narrowed to slivers. A hoarse roar erupted through his clenched teeth. "And then!" As he stood, his foot jammed the typewriter table and spun it around facing the wall. He raised the paperweight above his head and shook it. "And then what did you do to the idiot?"

Kroulik stared at his feet. The echo of Heilmann's roar faded away like the echo of a gong in an empty cathedral. At last their eyes met. Kroulik's voice rose just above a whisper. "Patzke was dead."

The color drained from Heilmann's face. The marble paperweight dropped from his hand to the desk, rolled onto the floor, and broke in two.

# GOLDEN BIRD

Martha Hauser brushed a strand of gray hair from her forehead and sighed. Two deep lines formed between her eyes. She laid a bundle of cotton in her lap and pushed her chair away from the spinning wheel in front of her. Just then a canary in a cage across the front room of the cabin began to sing. Mrs. Hauser smiled at the bird. "I'm glad Catherine insisted on bringing you when we moved from Pennsylvania," she said. "You sing like you haven't a care in the world!"

A shadow fell across the room. Startled, Mrs. Hauser glanced up to see Catherine carrying a wooden bowl filled with unshelled peas through the front door. The late afternoon sun shone through her long, golden hair. "This is all I could find in the garden today," the girl said as she drew a three-legged stool toward the spinning wheel. "I think there's time to shell them before we go to the fort." She lit a lantern, then smoothed her long, blue skirt with one hand. As Catherine began shelling the peas her mother sighed again and returned to her spinning. Neither spoke for a while.

At last Mrs. Hauser broke the silence. "Did you notice anything in the forest?" Her voice sounded tense.

Catherine shook her head, and the lines in her mother's face relaxed. "I saw the guard while I was in the garden," she said. "I'm sure he'll warn us if there's any danger. Besides, God is our True Guard, and nothing will happen to us that isn't a part of His plan. I'm sure He won't let anything harm us."

The Hausers and their fourteen-year-old daughter had settled on the frontier with a group of Christian families two years before. Nobody worried much about Indians then, so they built a fort, with their cabins in the clearing on the outside. Recently, though, the Indians all through the region had been restless, and several days before, word had reached the village that some were on the warpath, intent on ridding the land of its white settlers. The village council appointed a guard to watch the forest all day, and everyone slept in the fort at night.

Darkness had begun to settle over the land by the time Catherine finished the peas. She set them on a shelf beside the birdcage just as the canary began to sing again. Catherine leaned toward the cage and poked a finger inside. "What a pity you have to be a captive, little bird," she said. She thought a minute. "But if you weren't a captive, you couldn't sing to us about God's love, could you?"

Mrs. Hauser pushed the spinning wheel into one corner of the cabin. "We'd better go to the fort," she advised. She started to pick up the lantern, then cocked her head to one side. "I hear someone run-ning!" she exclaimed.

A man's face appeared in the door for an instant. "The Indians are coming!" he shouted, and he dashed to the next cabin.

"Run!" Mrs. Hauser screamed to her daughter. "Run for your life!"

Catherine started toward the door, then stopped. "My Bible!"

"No!" her mother cried, "there isn't time!" But Catherine had disappeared into the back room of the cabin. A second later she was back, clutching the black Book in her right hand. Mrs. Hauser ran out the door ahead of her. She heard the war cries of the Indians. All the way to the fort she kept glancing back, to be sure Catherine followed close behind. When she burst through the front gate, a wave of relief washed over her that they had made it in time. A large crowd of villagers milled about in the yard of the fort. The wild yells of the Indians reached the wall just as the gateman locked the gate. Soon arrows flew over the wall, and everyone ran for the cover of the church in the center of the stockade.

Suddenly the cries of the Indians ceased. As-tonished, the villagers looked at one another. Then they began searching for their family members. Mr. Hauser soon found his wife. "Where's Catherine?" he asked.

"Somewhere in the crowd," his wife replied. "She followed me into the fort." Not spotting her immediately, Mrs. Hauser pushed her way back and forth through the crowd. She kept calling "Catherine," but received no answer. Thoroughly alarmed, she found her husband again. "Catherine is *not* here!" Then she began wringing her hands. "She's gone! Catherine's gone!"

"Don't worry, we'll find her," her husband comforted.

But they didn't find Catherine. The settlers called a quick council and appointed three men to leave the fort with Mr. Hauser to hunt for his daughter. Mrs. Hauser insisted on going along. Carrying lanterns, they examined every inch of the way to the Hauser's cabin. They searched every corner of the cabin, but nowhere did they find the girl.

"Are you sure she left the cabin?" Mr. Hauser asked his wife.

She sank into her chair and buried her face in her hands. Her body shook, and she wept softly. "Oh, Catherine, my Catherine!" The canary chirped twice in its cage. Mrs. Hauser, raising her head, looked into her husband's face. Her lips quivered. "Catherine followed me out the door," she said, burying her face in her hands again.

Catherine had followed her mother out the door. But she had also dashed into the back room of the cabin, seized her Bible from a crude wooden table, and run back to her mother. She glanced at the forest as she burst through the front door. Dim shadows raced across the clearing toward the village. Startled that the Indians were so close, Catherine raised her skirt to her knees and dashed behind her mother toward the fort.

She had almost reached the gate when a stone struck the back of her head. Vaguely she was aware of falling and that the Bible flew from her hand as she sank to the ground. Strange voices that seemed far in the distance echoed in her ears. Strong arms seized her about the waist, and then she knew no more.

Red Raven had aimed carefully as he hurled the stone at the girl. Having seen the Bible drop from her hand, he picked it up before lifting her from the ground. Then he examined the wound the stone made. A trickle of blood from a deep gash on the back of her head stained her golden hair. The Indian put his ear against her back and listened. He grunted, raised her limp form over his shoulder, and trotted back toward the forest.

Halfway there he met Big Bounding Elk. They exchanged a few words, then the chief whistled shrilly and turned back to the woods. Red Raven followed him into thick undergrowth. Ten minutes later twenty-five war-painted Indians, talking excitedly, gathered about Catherine in the darkness.

Big Bounding Elk gave a sharp order. Red Raven raised Catherine to his shoulder again, and the Indians headed single file into the forest away from the village. Crickets chirped in the darkness. Owls hooted in the trees, and a coyote howled in the distance. Toward midnight the moon rose over the horizon and filtered its light through the trees onto the moss-covered forest floor. A light rain fell during the early morning hours.

The husky men took turns carrying Catherine through the night. From time to time the girl moaned and mumbled a few words, then sank back into unconsciousness. Shortly before dawn they reached a clearing beside a shallow stream. Red Raven laid Catherine on the grass, and they all sat down a short distance away to rest.

Catherine roused as the morning light began to creep across the eastern sky. She raised herself on one elbow. "Oh," she moaned, pressing her hand to the back of her head. She blinked her eyes and gazed about, wrinkling her forehead. "Where am I?" she wondered. She then saw the Indians. With a gasp, she shrank back from them. Red and black war paint covered their faces and chests. The braves wore leather girdles, and the chief wore a deerskin waistcoat.

Slowly the events of the evening before began to take shape in Catherine's mind. "What will they do to me?" she thought. "They'll harm me. Maybe they'll kill me! Or they'll take me away, and I'll never see my family again. I've got to get home. Father in heaven, help me."

After struggling to her feet, she stumbled toward the braves, who, motionless, expressionless, sat silently watching her. For a moment Catherine just looked back at them. Then she pointed into the forest. "Take me home." The Indians didn't move. "I said, 'Take me home!' " Still they didn't respond. Catherine realized that they didn't understand her, or that if they did, they had no intention of complying with her request.

Big Bounding Elk rose slowly to his feet, crossed his arms over his chest, and studied her intently, coldly, but not fiercely. The girl stared straight back into his dark eyes, her eyebrows lowered intently. Her heart pounded, her throat tightened. She wanted to scream, to weep, to fall at his feet and beg him to have mercy and return her to her family. But she knew that she dared not. Instead, she gazed into his face, at the high cheekbones, the firmly set jaw, the black hair that hung about his shoulders. They stood eyeing each other for two or three minutes.

Big Bounding Elk first broke the silence. He glanced at one of his braves and gave a short, sharp command. The Indian rose swiftly to his feet and bounded into the forest. Catherine wondered what the chief had said, but she no longer felt afraid. A few minutes later the brave returned with a bowl-shaped piece of bark in his hands. He strode to the river and filled the bark with water. Then he handed it to her.

Slowly Catherine took the bowl. "Th-thank you," she said quietly. She raised the edge of the bark to her lips and drank. The Indian returned to the river several times till she had had enough.

Catherine realized now that the Indians meant her no harm. "Thank you, God," she whispered. "And please make them take me home. Or help the men from the village to find me."

The men drew parched corn from pouches they carried and shared some with Catherine. She put one of the kernels in her mouth and shuddered. But it was the only food they had, and she managed to choke down enough to satisfy her hunger. Two of the braves hunted berries in the forest and brought them to her. She smiled and again thanked them. They grunted and walked away.

Big Bounding Elk barked another order, and the Indians gathered about him. He pointed to two saplings that stood about six feet apart at the edge of the forest, spoke a few words, and the braves scattered into the woods. Catherine's head began to ache again; so she sat on the grass and watched as they brought vines and strung them between the saplings. Then they began weaving other vines between them. Suddenly Catherine realized that they were fashioning a large net. "What are they going to do with it?" she wondered. Fear crept into her mind again. Would they put her in the net and tie her up and leave her? Would they drop her in the river to drown? What kind of prison were they weaving with the vines? "Dear God," she prayed, "please protect me from harm. And please help someone from the village to find me before it's too late!"

Apprehensively Catherine watched as the braves intertwined the last strand of vine into the net. Her anxiety for a time overcame the ache in the back of her head. She shrank back when they motioned for her to come. At Big Bounding Elk's signal one of the braves sprinted to her, picked her up in his arms, and carried her to the net. Terrified, she wanted to scream, but she held her breath. The Indian dropped her into the net.

Catherine shut her eyes and waited for the worst. She knew when the Indians removed the net from the saplings, and now she felt herself bouncing up and down as they walked away. Slowly she opened her eyes. The men walked single file through the forest. An Indian in front of her and one in back held the net. Suddenly she realized that they had made a crude hammock so she would not have to walk. "Thank You, God," she whispered, "for helping the Indians to be kind to me."

Closing her eyes again, Catherine rested. Pain throbbed in the back of her head. The hammock felt uncomfortable at best, especially with her headache. She began longing for home, thinking of the comfort of being with her parents and friends and of sleeping on a straw bed. Images flashed through her mind of her pet canary, and of shelling peas and mending clothes while she sat near her mother at the spinning wheel.

"Mother is crying for me," she thought. "She doesn't know whether I'm dead or alive. Father and a group of men are searching for me. God, please help them to find me. Don't let the Indians get too far away!"

Continuing to pray, Catherine watched the sun rise in the eastern sky. As they traveled farther and farther, a cold fear lurked in her mind: "Maybe they won't find me after all!" By the time the sun beat straight down, she realized that her captivity was absolute and that there would be no deliverance. Hopelessness swept over her then. She knew that she must make her way in life alone, a prisoner among a strange people who were enemies of her race. Burying her face in her arm so the Indians would not see, she wept. "O God," she cried, "Why? Why? Why? Why must I be captured like an animal, trapped like a bird in a cage? Where were You last night when the Indians attacked our village? Why must this happen to me?"

For several hours Catherine gave herself up to despair. Her mind burned with agony, and her weeping never ceased. By midafternoon she was so exhausted from nervous strain that she fell asleep. Feeling better when she awoke, she began to think of the future—not as she wanted it but as apparently it must now be. What she could not change, she decided, she must accept. Slowly a new thought began to form in her mind. Maybe this *was* God's plan for her life. Hadn't she told her mother just the day before that God would allow nothing to happen to them that was not a part of His will? The girl remembered Joseph, taken captive from his home to a strange land, and of the great mission he fulfilled for God. She thought of Jesus, who, in order that He might save them, left heaven to live among a people who finally killed Him. The words He had spoken came to her: "Love your enemies."

Catherine determined that captivity would not mean the end of her usefulness or of her happiness. It would mean the beginning of a new service to God in a new place. "Dear God," she now prayed, "help me to do Your work wherever I may be. Help me to witness Your love to these people and win some of them to You."

Quietly Catherine prayed in her hammock the rest of the afternoon. Toward sunset the party stopped for the night in a small clearing by a creek. Several of the Indians built a fire. The rest caught fish, which they wrapped in mud and laid in the fire to cook. Again they shared their meal with Catherine, who by now had gone for more than twenty-four hours with nothing more than a few kernels of parched corn.

Soon everyone had eaten his fill. Sitting on a grassy spot, Catherine busied herself with her thoughts and failed to notice that the Indians had gathered quietly in a circle about her. Big Bounding Elk grunted, and Catherine glanced up. "Oh!" she gasped, throwing her hand to her mouth. She looked from one to the other. They did not smile, but neither did she see anger or threats in their faces.

Big Bounding Elk reached inside his deerskin waistcoat and drew out a small, black object.

"My Bible!" Catherine cried, springing to her feet.

Big Bounding Elk walked slowly to her and handed her the Book.

"Oh, thank you!" she exclaimed. She clutched the Book to her breast. Then she knelt on the ground and raised her arms toward heaven. "Thank You, dear God. Thank You for preserving Your Word for me in my captivity."

When she had finished praying, Catherine noticed the Indians had fallen back and now whispered quietly among themselves, casting guarded glances at her and the Book. She realized that they felt a sense of awe in her presence and in that of the Bible, as though the Book held some supernatural power that they did not understand.

All that night Catherine slept in her hammock. Before dawn the next morning the Indians went on their way again. For seven days she rode farther and farther from home. She still longed for her own people, and sometimes she wept and prayed that God would somehow deliver her. But she spent most of the time reading the Bible and thinking of the new life God had opened up to her. "I must learn their ways," she told herself. "I must become an Indian too. Then perhaps they will listen as I tell them of the true God and His Son."

On the eighth day the Indians started earlier, and they seemed to walk faster than usual. About noon they crossed a river and stopped. They motioned for Catherine to get out of the hammock, after which they cast it into the forest. She followed them along a trail that led through the trees up the side of a mountain. Fifteen minutes later they broke into a clearing, and Big Bounding Elk gave a long, shrill whistle. Instantly shouts filled the forest, and in a few seconds men, women, and children surrounded the returning warriors. The braves whooped and yelled and did a ceremonial dance before their families and friends.

Catherine shrank into the edge of the clearing. For several minutes nobody noticed her. Then a child pointed her way and screamed. The villagers fell back at sight of the white girl, and the forest became silent. Big Bounding Elk approached Catherine and motioned for her to come into the clearing. Then all the Indians surrounded her, everyone chattering at once. They touched her dress, examined her shoes, and passed their hands lightly, delicately, over her white skin as though they feared it would rub off on their fingers. Several of them peered into her eyes and pointed to the sky. But they seemed most fascinated by her long, golden hair. The women and girls stroked it with their hands and ran it through their fingers.

One of the braves pointed to Catherine's Bible, then spoke to the people. When a hush fell over the group, Catherine realized that the whole village felt the same sense of awe in her presence that she had seen in the braves a few days before. Kneeling, she raised her arms to heaven with her Bible in her right hand. "Dear Father," she prayed in a quiet voice, but loud enough that the Indians could hear. "These people already respect Thy Word and me, Thy messenger. Help me to honor their trust, and give me some of them for Thy kingdom. Amen." Then she bowed her head and folded her hands over her breast for several seconds.

The Indians said nothing when she arose. For a long time they watched. After a while a few of them began to whisper. Big Bounding Elk called out something, and a girl about Catherine's own age stepped from the circle. The warrior led her to Catherine and spoke two words. The girl repeated the words and stroked Catherine's long, golden hair. Then she smiled and took Catherine's hand as though to lead her away. The white girl followed.

The two girls walked up the side of the mountain. A few minutes later Catherine spotted Indian houses among the tall birch and aspen trees in the forest. Built on poles, they stood about four feet off the ground. Mud plastered their outsides, and some of them had been painted with a white, chalky substance. The Indian girl led the way up a crude ladder into one of them. Around the inside wall Catherine noticed a low shelf. The girl lay down on the shelf on one side, then took Catherine to the other side and pointed to the one there. When Catherine lay down and the girl smiled, she decided that this must be her place to sleep, and that the girl was to be her companion. The Indian girl brought several kernels of parched corn and handed them to Catherine. She seemed pleased when the white girl ate them.

Quickly Catherine learned that the words the Indian girl had spoken that first day in the forest when she stroked her hair were her Indian name. She knew that Indian names always meant something.

The two became friends. The Indian girl seemed eager to teach Catherine her language. She would point to a tree, a blade of grass, or a stone, and say a word. Catherine always repeated it after her till she had memorized it. After a few days she began picking up snatches of conversation, and within a few weeks she could talk, after a fashion, in the Indian dialect. She also learned how the Indian women cooked, how they cured their leather, and how they

made their garments. Soon she had made for herself
an entire outfit of Indian clothing, and she put aside
forever the dress she had worn at her capture. "I
wish I had a mirror," she mused to herself one day.
"I'd like to see what a fine-looking Indian I really
must be!"

Every morning Catherine took her Bible to a
quiet spot in the forest to read and pray. At first the
Indians followed her to see where she went. When
she had finished reading, she always knelt and
raised her arms to heaven with her Bible in her right
hand, praying out loud in her own English language. Sometimes she spoke in the Indian dialect
also, especially after she had learned it well enough
to converse. At times she missed her old home
terribly and would then beg God, during her
morning devotions, to bring her back to her family.

Catherine noticed that the Indians, even Chief
Big Bounding Elk, seemed to have a special respect
for her that was different, and in some ways
greater, from that toward any other leader among
their people. They never disturbed her in her devotions, and they always whispered quietly among
themselves when she returned.

Eventually Catherine learned that her friend's
name meant Gray Fawn. She always responded
when someone called her own new name, but she
wondered what it meant. One morning as she returned from her devotions in the forest she heard a
child say her name. When she turned, to her surprise she discovered that the little boy didn't seem
to be addressing her at all. Instead, he stood point-

ing into a birch tree overhead. Curious, Catherine walked over and peered into the branches of the tree. Perched on a limb, perhaps halfway up in the tree, a yellow finch trilled its song. The bird stopped singing when Catherine approached and cocked its head first one way, then the other, watching her with its tiny black eyes. Then it darted from the branch and flew away. The little Indian boy laughed and clapped his hands, and repeated Catherine's Indian name again.

"So that's it!" Catherine said to herself as she walked toward her house. "My name is the same as the yellow finch. It means 'golden bird.' It must be because of my hair."

Several weeks went by. One morning Catherine and Gray Fawn sat in front of their house, pounding corn into meal on two grinding logs. From a large basket between them Catherine took kernels of dried corn and dropped them into the hollow in the center of her log. She crushed the corn with a smaller, rounded piece of wood that she held in her hand. When the corn had become a fine powder, she scooped the meal into an earthen pot.

The two girls laughed and chatted for perhaps half an hour. Then Gray Fawn became silent. Catherine wondered what she was thinking about. "Does Golden Bird know the Great Spirit?" Gray Fawn asked at last.

Catherine's heart leaped, and she took a short, quick breath. "God, help me to answer Gray Fawn right," she asked Him under her breath. "Give me words to reach her heart." Then she turned to her friend. "Yes, Golden Bird knows the Great Spirit."

Gray Fawn pondered Catherine's answer a long time. "We see you talk to the sky each morning in the forest. We think you talk to the Great Spirit. Now I will tell the people that you do!"

Bringing her Bible from their house, she handed it to Gray Fawn. The Indian girl's eyes widened and she shrank back.

"Go ahead and hold it," Catherine urged with a smile. Cautiously Gray Fawn reached out and took the Book. Catherine helped her open it. "This is a message from the Great Spirit to Golden Bird," she said. "The Great Spirit has told us all about Himself in this message." She took the Bible from Gray Fawn's hands and began to read, translating as best she could from English into the Indian language: "The Great Spirit made the heavens and the earth at the first," she began. "The earth was empty. There was nothing in it." She read through the entire first chapter of Genesis and explained how God made the world and man.

The Indian girl thought about what Catherine had read. "There are many spirits," she said.

"There is one Great Spirit," Catherine replied. "He has a Son and a Helper. The Great Spirit sends us the sunshine and the rain."

Gray Fawn nodded. "He sends the deer for us to hunt and the fish for us to catch for food."

The two girls talked about God the rest of the morning. The subject did not come up again for several days, except in occasional comments that Gray Fawn made. Catherine prayed that God

would open the way for her to speak to Gray Fawn
again about the Bible and the true God, and she
continued her daily devotional time in the woods.

Several months passed, and the two girls came
to the place that they talked freely about God. Gray
Fawn especially enjoyed listening as Catherine
read to her from the Bible and explained what it
meant. One evening, shortly before dusk, Gray
Fawn and Golden Bird sat in front of their house
discussing Jesus and His death. They had talked
only a few minutes when they heard footsteps of
someone hurrying toward them in the dark. A
young brave ran up to their house somewhat out of
breath. "Golden Bird," he panted, "Chief Big
Bounding Elk wants to see you at the council fire
tonight. You must come now."

Catherine caught her breath. "What does the
chief want with me?" she wondered, but said nothing. She followed the young man through the village. The moonlight fell in splotches through the
trees. Light from the fire glowed through the cracks
in the council house as they approached the center
of the village. The building was partially sunk in
the ground. The guide led Catherine down an in-
cline, through a door, into a smoke-filled room. The
chief and his counselors sat on logs in the far end of
the circular chamber. A fire burned in the center of
the room. Beside it, stuck in the ground, stood a tall
pole that reached almost to the ceiling. A stuffed
eagle sat on top of the pole that was near an opening
in the center of the roof where the smoke was supposed to escape. The white girl's guide led her to a

log near the fire. She sat down facing the village leaders. Big Bounding Elk rose, arms folded, and gazed at her. He wore a deerskin coat with beads woven into the breast, and he had a tomahawk pushed into the girdle about his waist. Catherine saw neither friendliness nor hostility in his face. After a few seconds he spoke. "Golden Bird, your sister, Gray Fawn, tells us that you know the Great Spirit. She says that He sent you a message in the black words you brought when you came to the village. Tell us of the Great Spirit."

Through the opening in the center of the roof Catherine saw several stars twinkling in the sky. "Dear Father," she breathed, "show me what to say." Then she faced Big Bounding Elk. "The Great Spirit has a message for the chief and his counselors. You must treat all men as brothers."

"All men do not treat *us* as brothers," the chief replied. "The white man drives us from our land and gives us nothing in return."

Catherine pondered before replying. "Golden Bird is sorry that her white brothers do not always treat the Indians like their brothers. Our white brothers are wrong. They do not obey the Great Spirit."

The counselors nodded their heads and murmured. Catherine noticed the chief's stern face relax a bit. After a moment he looked at her again. "How many spirits are there?" he asked.

"There are three chief Spirits in the heavens. The Great Spirit is our Father. He has a Son and a Partner."

One of the counselors frowned at her. "There are *many* spirits!" he hissed.

"Big Bounding Elk's adviser speaks wise words," Catherine responded. "The Great Spirit has many other spirits to be His messengers. When the braves go on the hunt, these spirits help their arrows to find many deer, and they protect the braves from harm."

Again the counselors murmured their approval. One of them motioned with his hand. Big Bounding Elk gave him permission to speak. "There are also evil spirits that do us harm," he said. "They keep back the rain, and they bring sickness and death to our houses."

"It is true," Catherine agreed. "There are many evil spirits. But they were not always evil. Many seasons ago they were among the beloved spirit messengers who did good. Then the chief of the messenger spirits rebelled against the Father Spirit and His Son. Many other messengers followed him. These are the ones who now do us harm."

The group of men before Catherine turned to one another and began discussing among themselves in low tones. After a few minutes Big Bounding Elk spoke to her again. "The black words, the message that the Great Spirit has sent to Golden Bird, are they full of magic?"

Her eyebrows drew together before she spoke. "The black words by which the Great Spirit speaks to Golden Bird are very powerful."

"Do they make us well when we are sick?" the chief asked.

"If that is the Father Spirit's will. But the black words are especially powerful to make all men treat each other as brothers. They turn men who kill into men who protect even those who want to destroy them."

"Do they make the Indian help the white man?" one of the counselors questioned.

Catherine sensed a note of skepticism in his words, but she nodded.

The Indian who had spoken rose to his feet and glared. He spat back his reply. "But they don't make the white man help the Indian!" Scorn and hate hardened his voice. He whirled and stalked out of the council room. The other Indians stood and began talking rapidly among themelves. Big Bounding Elk motioned to Catherine's guide, and he ushered her back to her house.

Gray Fawn had already gone to sleep when Catherine climbed the ladder and entered the dark room. Quickly Catherine prepared for bed. "Dear God," she prayed when she had lain down, "the Indians don't *want* to hear about You. I'm a white woman, an enemy of their race. How can *I* tell them about You? Won't You please let me go back to my family? It's *so* hard without them."

Tears streamed down her face, and for a time she again surrendered to despair. Then the text, "He came unto his own, and his own received him not," passed through her mind. She thought of the prejudice Jesus faced on earth. "At least they haven't threatened to kill me," she thought. "Forgive me, Lord, for doubting the power of Your Word to

change their hard hearts. Show me how to teach
them, and make my life an example of the words I
speak.''

In the days that followed, Catherine noticed that
the Indians still treated her with great awe and
respect. Even Big Bounding Elk, who never smiled,
seemed to show more interest in her. Daily he
brought food for her and Gray Fawn. Sometimes he
paused and asked her a few questions before he
went on his way. Once he even inquired if she liked
her new home in the village. She smiled and said,
''Yes.'' He grunted and walked on. Afterward she
wondered why he had asked.

Constantly Catherine prayed that God would
open the way for her to soon see her loved ones
again. She especially wished that she had someone
she could talk to about Big Bounding Elk. He was
handsome and attentive in an Indian's way.
Catherine noticed the Indian girls casting envious
glances toward her when Big Bounding Elk brought
food. Sometimes he just visited, and although he
talked mostly to Gray Fawn, Catherine knew it was
not the Indian girl he had come to see.

By now Catherine had lived in the Indian village
two years, perhaps a bit longer. She and Gray Fawn
discussed God and the Bible every day. And Big
Bounding Elk asked her quite frequently to the
council house to talk to his counselors about the
Great Spirit and the black words. Catherine wondered whether anything would ever come of it,
though. Gray Fawn seemed most receptive, and
some of the counselors responded favorably. But

other counselors and some of the villagers opposed her religion strongly, even bitterly. Although Big Bounding Elk's thinking seemed to sway from one side to the other, Catherine took courage in the fact that he kept inviting her to the council. "If only he would take a firm stand for God, I know others would follow," she repeated over and over to herself.

One morning when Catherine woke up, she thought she heard more activity outside than usual. Gray Fawn was already moving about their house. "There is to be a village council today," Gray Fawn said when she saw that the white girl was awake. Something about the way Gray Fawn spoke made Catherine catch her breath. Later in the morning as the two girls followed the other villagers through the trees to the council house, Catherine noticed the Indians casting glances at her and whispering among themselves. "I wonder what's so important about the council meeting today," she pondered.

The council room was packed when Catherine and Gray Fawn entered, but the Indians around the door pressed aside and made an aisle for them down to the front of the room, before the fire. Catherine's heart beat faster. She wondered if the chief had called the entire village together to hear a message from the Bible. Perhaps he intended to indicate his own feelings more positively today.

All the villagers murmured when Big Bounding Elk and his counselors arrived. They filed to the center and took their places about the fire. Big Bounding Elk stood up. Catherine noticed that he was dressed in a brand-new waistcoat. His long black hair shone with bear grease. The chief raised his right arm, and the crowd hushed. "My people," he said, "we have brought Golden Bird to rest in our village. The white man has many golden birds, and he will not miss this one. Golden Bird is welcome here. Words of wisdom are in her mouth. It is good that she has become a sister to Gray Fawn."

Catherine's heart pounded as Big Bounding Elk spoke.

"Big Bounding Elk is alone in his cabin," the chief continued. "He has no mate. Let Golden Bird come to his house and be his mate. Then he shall rule his people with greater wisdom, and he will lead them to better hunting grounds. Golden Bird will teach us great wisdom from the black words. The white man shall be our brother, and we shall all be one people. The chief has spoken."

The girl trembled. Her arms and legs seemed to lose their strength, and her head felt faint. She felt everyone's eyes fixed on her. For a moment she turned her face toward heaven. "Dear God, what shall I say?" she breathed. Then she rose to her feet.

Raising her arms, Catherine studied the people before her. "My people—for you *are* my people— the Great Spirit has sent me to you." She pointed heavenward as she spoke, then continued, "I love you all. Your chief is good. He will lead you to good hunting grounds. He will protect you from the enemies of the forest.

"Golden Bird is the chief's sister, for she is the sister of Gray Fawn, who is also his sister. Golden

Bird would not be happy living in the house of Big Bounding Elk as his mate, for he is her brother. The Great Spirit would be displeased if Golden Bird should become the mate of her brother. He would take Golden Bird away. Then you would not learn wisdom from the black words. So Golden Bird will continue to live with her red sister, and she will continue to teach her red brothers wisdom from the Great Spirit's black words. Golden Bird has spoken, and her red brothers will hear."

The council room buzzed as Catherine sat down, and she saw nods of approval everywhere. Big Bounding Elk stood and motioned toward the door. The crowd parted. Gray Fawn took Catherine's hand and led the way out into the fresh air and sunshine.

When they returned home, Catherine told Gray Fawn that she wanted to be alone for a while. When the Indian girl had gone, she flung herself onto her sleeping platform and wept. "O God!" she cried. "I want a home of my own, a husband and children to love. Why must I be a captive in this strange village, among enemies of my own people? Why can't I live with my friends back home?" Then the verse, "The Word was made flesh, and dwelt among us," passed through her mind. She sat up and dried her tears. "And I must be made an Indian so I can witness to the Indians," she whispered. "Forgive me, Lord, for doubting." She knew, though, that she could not become the chief's wife, for since she would then be subordinate to him, it would weaken her influence with the tribe.

Big Bounding Elk continued to bring food daily to the two girls, but he seldom stayed more than a few minutes, and he talked mostly to Gray Fawn when he did. He always treated Catherine with respect though, and more and more he requested her to speak about God to his men around the council fire. She taught them about Jesus, of His rejection by His own people, and of His death for them and for all men. Seldom did she see approving glances among the men around the council fire, and sometimes there came sharp words of disapproval, but Gray Fawn told her that the things she said were strongly influencing some of the men.

Time went on, and Catherine not only taught the villagers about God but also sat with the counselors as they made plans for the people. On several occasions, when the leaders planned war with a neighboring tribe, Catherine led the Indians to find a peaceful settlement with their enemies. " 'Blessed are the peacemakers: for they shall be called the children of God,' " she said over and over again.

Months passed by, and Catherine lost track of the time, though she knew when the years came and went as winter turned to spring and summer again.

One day Catherine noticed little knots of people gathered here and there about the village. She felt tension in the air, and she knew that something important would soon happen. But always when she approached a group of people chattering excitedly, they hushed and dispersed. From the behavior of the braves she knew that the tribe intended a war. "I wonder if they are planning to attack a white man's village," she asked herself several times through the day. She determined to find out.

A small fire burned in a clay pot that evening as Catherine and Gray Fawn prepared to settle down for the night. Catherine noticed that Gray Fawn seemed more restless than usual. She moved rapidly about the cabin, yet her movements seemed almost pointless at times, and she obviously did not want to look Catherine in the eye. When Gray Fawn reached to put out the fire for the night, Catherine grasped her hand. "My sister has news in her eyes," Catherine said.

Gray Fawn fixed her gaze on the burning embers and remained silent.

"The warriors are preparing for battle," Catherine persisted. "Around which white brother's camp will they gather tonight?"

Gray Fawn gasped. "How did you know?" she exclaimed under breath.

"The Great Spirit has helped Golden Bird to know. If Gray Fawn will tell me, I will keep it a secret."

The Indian girl stared into the fire again before she spoke. "Gray Fawn is not supposed to tell. The white man sleeps in wagons on the other side of the mountain." She motioned toward the mountaintop with her hand. "The white man has come a long way, but he will go no farther. My people will attack. They will get many scalps. Afterward they will bring many white children to the village, and

Golden Bird will have white brothers and sisters."
Gray Fawn pointed upward. "When the moon is
high, they go."

Swallowing hard, Catherine tightened the knot
that formed in her stomach. But she kept a calm
expression on her face. "Golden Bird is sorry," she
said. She reached for Gray Fawn's hand and gave it
a gentle squeeze. "The Great Spirit will bring
peace."

Catherine lay on her bed till she heard Gray
Fawn's breathing come slow and heavy. Then she
slipped into her moccasins. Draping a dark blanket
around her white doeskin garment, she slipped out
the door and down the steps into the cool night air.
A thick darkness covered the village. She tiptoed to
a bush near the cabin and crouched beside it.

Toward midnight the moon rose over the land,
casting patches of light onto the ground through the
leaves in the trees. Catherine heard what seemed to
be an owl hoot in the center of the village. Then
came another, and a moment later another closer
by. The leaves rustled on the trail beside her cabin,
and a brave passed by. He was so close she could
hear his moccasins pad on the ground. Again
Catherine heard the owl hoot, and seeing that it
came from the brave, she knew that it was a signal.

When she felt certain that the last of the warriors
had passed by, Catherine slipped through the
shadows to the center of the village. She hid behind
another bush where she could watch the entrance to
the council chamber.

Light from the fire flickered through the door-

way, and a thin column of smoke shone in the
moonlight as it rose from the hole in the roof.
Voices, some low, others louder, came from the
building. Ten minutes later two dozen Indians filed
out and started up the trail toward the top of the
mountain. Gathering her dark blanket about her
shoulders, Catherine quietly followed them. The
braves disappeared into the forest.

Moonlight shone in patches on the forest floor.
The chill night air closed in about them, and
Catherine felt thankful for the warmth that her
blanket provided. She peered into the darkness,
trying to let the Indians stay as far ahead of her as
possible, but not so far that she would lose them.
Most of the time she could see the shadows of the
last few warriors among the trees. Occasionally a
large patch of moonlight broke across the trail, giv-
ing her a clear view. Big Bounding Elk, the chief in
the lead, gave an occasional owl hoot, and the Indian bringing up the rear always hooted back. This,
and the cracking of a twig under their feet now and
then, helped her to keep up without being de-
tected.

When the moon disappeared behind a cloud,
Catherine found it almost impossible to see. "Dear
God," she prayed, "guide my steps so I won't lose
my way." Sometimes she felt that Someone else
walked beside her, in answer to her prayer, show-
ing her where to go. An hour passed, and Catherine
began to feel the strain of the continual climb, for
she followed men used to long hikes. She began
praying for strength, too.

A few minutes later the trail emerged from the trees and wound along the wall of a cliff. The mountain fell off at a steep angle below. After a short distance the trail veered sharply upward and to the right, between two massive boulders, and broke onto the mountain's crest. Catherine gasped as she gazed across the wide plain below. Patches of mist hung here and there over the valley, shimmering in the full light of the moon. And in the distance she saw several specks of orange light in a cluster. "The fires of the pioneers!" she said under her breath. Her heart leaped within her as she realized that this night, for the first time in many years, she would see white men and women, the people of her own race. "Dear God," she breathed in prayer, "is this to be the night of my deliverance from captivity?"

The sight on the plain so entranced Catherine that she momentarily forgot the war party she trailed. The sound of an owl hoot in the forest below brought her back to reality. She drew the dark blanket closer over her head and hurried after them. The downward path was much easier to follow and much swifter. The Indians trotted most of the way. Half an hour later the forest stopped abruptly at the foot of the mountain. The plain descended in a gentle slope ahead. The fires of the wagon train burned only half a mile ahead. Catherine's heart pounded, and her mouth went dry. White people! People who could understand her language, who could laugh when she laughed and cry when she cried.

But those same white people whom she longed

to join were about to be massacred, arrows piercing
their hearts, the hair torn from their skulls, their
blood spilled to mingle with the dust on which they
now slept. "O God," she cried out in her heart,
"why cannot the white man and the Indian live
together like brothers in the same land? Why can
they not stop being enemies, stop this revenge—
this killing—and be friends?"

For an instant all of her efforts of the past few
years to teach the Indians to love the white man
passed through her mind. She knew the injustice of
the white man to the Indian, that as often as not he
deserved the punishment he got. But she realized,
too, that the power of God could work in the heart
of the Indian to help him forgive. Catherine determined that this night, with God's help, she would
fulfill her mission.

The braves had huddled together when they
reached the plain, and Catherine could hear their
low voices as they planned their attack. Now they
split, one group creeping off to the right, the other
to the left. Catherine waited till she could no longer
hear the tall grass rustle under their feet. Then she
drew the blanket over her head, crouched low over
the prairie, and sped straight for the fires ahead.
She heard an owl hoot to her left. An answer came
from the right. Racing forward, she tried to keep up
with the signals on either side.

Now she could make out the shapes of the wagons surrounding the fires. Somewhere a dog
barked in the camp, and a gruff voice snapped,
"Shut up!" A man in a red shirt held a rifle across

his shoulder with one hand and stirred the fire with the other. Sparks mingled with the smoke and drifted toward the sky. Creeping up to the nearest wagon, Catherine rested against its wheel. The man set his rifle aside and threw a pile of sticks into the flames. The embers crackled, and a shower of sparks scattered about the fire. The flames leaped higher for a few seconds, then settled back down again.

A cricket chirped beside her, and a breeze rustled the leaves. The owl hoots sounded closer as the braves neared the camp. The dog tensed, pointed its ears toward the hoots on the left, and growled. Catherine took a deep breath, and for an instant she closed her eyes. "God, don't let it happen!" she breathed.

A terrible cry pierced the air. The man at the fire leaped for his gun and fired a wild shot into the sky. Two dozen white men with rifles in their hands burst from the hoods over the wagons. An arrow hit the side of the wagon where Catherine stood, and inside a woman shrieked. Another arrow flew into the fire and sent a shower of sparks into the air. The Indian warriors rushed into the camp.

Wrapping her body with her blanket, Catherine leaped over the tongue of the wagon and hurtled toward the fire. An arrow grazed her back. A rifle butt smashed into her head. She realized that neither the white men nor the Indians knew who she was. Dashing up to the fire, she leaped into the air and flung the dark mantle from her shoulder. The light from the fire glowed on her white doeskin garments, and as she fell to the earth she appeared almost like an apparition, a spirit from heaven.

Catherine held her Bible high in the air and shouted, "No!" The command of her voice rang through the camp. Instantly the noise of battle ceased. The white men stood petrified with fear. The astonished Indians dropped their weapons and gazed upon the beautiful being that seemed to have dropped from the sky. The light of the fire glowed in her golden hair. Fearlessness and power flashed from her eyes. Her gaze pierced everyone.

"The Great Spirit says no!" Catherine said in the Indian tongue. "The red man and the white man are brothers. The great God has sent me to tell you that you must not kill. Blood must not flow between the red brother and his white brother. They shall be friends." Again she pointed toward the heavens. "The Great Spirit commands!"

The confused braves clustered about their chief. Big Bounding Elk stood before Catherine with his head bowed. When he glanced up, she fixed her eyes on his. Then she slowly raised one arm and pointed back toward the mountain. "Go!" she ordered in a low voice. "The Great Spirit will guide you. Big Bounding Elk will lead his braves back to the village. The white man will stay here in safety."

The chief said nothing, made no move to leave. His bow and arrows hung loosly from his hands, and he searched Catherine's face. Neither of them spoke. The white men stood speechless, terrified, dumbfounded, by the drama that opened before them.

The battle in the camp had ceased, but one still raged in Catherine's heart. She glanced at the white men before her, at the women and children cringing in the shadows of the wagons. A longing rose up within her once more to live among the people of her birth. Then she turned to the Indians to whom she had dedicated her life, among whom God had placed her to live, and whom she had grown to love. Big Bounding Elk continued to study her. Catherine caught her breath, then raised her arm and pointed again toward the mountain. "Go," she said quietly, "and Golden Bird will follow. Her home will be in the village with her red brothers."

The chief stood straight and tall. He dropped his weapons and folded his arms over his breast. His expression softened, and for the first time in her life, Catherine saw a smile on his face. Turning to his braves, he quietly spoke one word to them, and they slipped out of the camp toward the mountain. When he glanced at Catherine, she smiled at him.

The white settlers now began to regain their composure. The man in the red shirt, the guard that Catherine had seen tending the fire, asked, "Are you a captive, Miss?"

Catherine did not reply immediately. "Not a captive now," she answered, "but an honored friend and counselor, a member of this Indian tribe. It is by choice that I am God's messenger to our red brothers. They need me. I go to their council fires and teach them of the true God, the Great Spirit who leads all men to be brothers. You may rest in peace here tonight and continue on your journey tomorrow. May the loving Father ever watch over you. In return for the service I have rendered to you tonight, I ask only that you show kindness to the red brothers whom you meet. They always remember a kindness, and they never forget an injury. We who know of God's goodness should make known His loving-kindness to these, our brothers, who know Him not."

Gathering up the blanket she had dropped to the ground, Catherine raised herself to her full height and gazed once more upon the white people whose lives she had spared and to whom she had once longed to return. "Good night," she said. As she passed through their midst into the darkness outside the camp Big Bounding Elk followed.

The two walked alone across the prairie toward the mountain, their feet rustling in the grass. The crickets ahead stopped chirping as they approached. An owl hoot sounded in the distance, but Big Bounding Elk did not reply. Grasping her arm instead, he stopped and turned her toward him. Their eyes met before he spoke. "Big Bounding Elk has found new brothers tonight," he told her. "In my village the white man and the red man are one, as the Great Spirit says."

Golden Bird's eyes filled with tears, and she bowed her head. "Thank You, God," she whispered. Then she looked back up at her chief. "Come, we must find our red brothers and return to our village on the other side of the mountain."